MW00329837

Dunwich's Guide
to
GEMSTONE
SORCERY

Using Stones for
Spells, Amulets, Rituals,
and Divination

Gerina Dunwich

New Page Books
A division of The Career Press, Inc.
Franklin Lakes, NJ

DUNWICH'S GUIDE TO GEMSTONE SORCERY
EDITED AND TYPESET BY CLAYTON W. LEADBETTER
Cover design by Diane Y. Chin
Printed in the U.S.A. by Book-mart Press

To order this title, please call toll-free 1-800-CAREER-1 (NJ and Canada: 201-848-0310) to order using VISA or MasterCard, or for further information on books from Career Press.

The Career Press, Inc., 3 Tice Road, PO Box 687,
Franklin Lakes, NJ 07417
www.careerpress.com
www.newpagebooks.com

Library of Congress Cataloging-in-Publication Data

Dunwich, Gerina.
    Dunwich's guide to gemstone sorcery : using stones for spells,
amulets, rituals, and divination / by Gerina Dunwich.
        p. cm.
    Includes bibliographical references (p.) and index.
    ISBN 1-56414-672-3 (pbk.)
        1. Gems—Miscellanea. 2. Precious stones—Psychic aspects. 3. Magic.
    I. Title: Guide to gemstone sorcery. II. Title.

BF1442.P74D86 2003
133'.25538—dc21

2003045938

Dedication

With love and gratitude, I dedicate this book to my mother and Al Jackter.

Acknowledgments

I wish to thank my agent, Stephany Evans; my editor, Clayton Leadbetter; and my publisher, Ron Fry, for helping to make this book possible. And very special thanks to my dear friend, Lee Prosser, for his wonderful contribution of Witch Stones; and to the Rev. Judith Lewis of the New Moon Occult Shop for her contribution of A Dragon Love Spell and Dream Spell (To Dream of a Certain Person). Blessed be!

Contents

Foreword

he word *sorcery* is said to have originated sometime in the
14th century and hails from the Latin *sortiri*, which means, "to
cast lots." According to *Webster's New Encyclopedia of Dictionaries*,
it means "witchcraft; magic; enchantment." The Merriam-
Webster's Collegiate Dictionary defines it as "magic—an extraordinary power or influence seemingly from a supernatural
source." However, a more insightful definition is offered by
Nicholas Hall, author of the book, *Chaos and Sorcery*, who
refers to it as "the art of using base materials to enhance a
magical conjuration, the outcome of which is determined by
the sorcerer's will."

When the base materials that come into play are composed of precious and semiprecious stones, the art can then be
classified as gemstone sorcery—one of the oldest forms of
magick known to mankind. And being that it is also the most
simplistic, it is one that calls to many individuals who find
themselves drawn to the mysterious and magickal energies of
stones.

The power of gemstone sorcery is essentially set into motion by a fusing of the natural receptive or projective energies of the stones, the will and intent of the magician, and the planetary, astrological, and elemental influences. It can work for good or evil (depending upon one's intent) and can yield either subtle or dramatic results, depending upon the intensity of energy that one weaves into the fabric of his or her spellwork.

With a good understanding of the workings of magick, along with a bit of practice (which is essential to the development of one's magickal skills), nearly anyone with good visualization skills and conviction can transform themselves into a gemstone sorcerer or sorceress in a relatively short amount of time.

Gemstone Sorcery
by Gerina Dunwich

Gemstones of sorcery,
Charms of the Earth,
To magick and mystery
They giveth birth.

Jewels of enchantment,
Majestic and bold,
Primordial wisdom and
Secrets they hold.

Weareth their brilliance
In pendant or crown,
Then greatness and power
Shall be your renown.

Introduction

From Stone Age to New Age

he energy contained within stones is a mysterious and invisible power that is as old as the Earth itself—perhaps even older. It is known throughout the world by many names and has been utilized by countless practitioners of divination and the magickal arts since the most primitive of times. It is an energy that, when properly harnessed, can enable a person to create powerful transformations and reconnect with the magick of Mother Nature and the Earth.

Ceremonial magicians have long valued certain gemstones as ritual tools for summoning, as well as for banishing spiritual entities and demonic forces. Many of the ancient grimoires speak of the numerous ways in which stones can be made to serve magicians. However, their most common usage lies in the form of amulets and talismans to ward off bad luck and evil influences, to obtain wealth, to fan the flames of love, to obtain occult knowledge, to gain mastery over others, to conjure visions of things that are yet to be, and to cast, as well as to reverse, curses. In the right hands, stones (especially crystals) can also act as powerful instruments for the healing of one's body, mind, and spirit.

I am firmly of the opinion that certain stones are meant to work for certain individuals. When the time is right (and only nature or deity can decide this) a stone that is destined to be in your life for some reason will find its way to you. It may arrive innocently as a gift from a caring friend or a loved one, perhaps in the form of jewelry. It may suddenly make itself known to you while you are strolling down the seashore, hiking in the mountains, or walking a path meandering through the woodlands. Or, as so often turns out to be the case, your eyes may focus on a particular stone in a gift shop, a rock shop, or a place that carries metaphysical supplies, and suddenly feel powerfully drawn to it—perhaps due to the unique shape or color of the stone, or because of the way it feels (or, perhaps, the way it makes you feel) when you touch or hold it in your hand. It is also not unusual for some persons to find themselves greatly attracted to a particular stone for no apparent reason other than feeling compelled to have it in their possession. In such instances, one should always allow his or her natural intuition and instincts to serve as a guide.

On the other hand, should a stone that finds its way into your life make you feel ominous in any way or affect you in a negative manner, such as by creating within you feelings of uneasiness, depression, or even physical illness, it would probably be to your advantage to promptly return the stone to the place from whence it came, give it to someone whose personal energies are more compatible with it, cast it into the sea, or bury it deep within the earth in a place far from where you live.

Whatever method you choose to dispose of a "bad" stone is not of the greatest importance. Keep in mind that the main objective in this case is for you to simply be rid of it, along with whatever negative vibrations may be emanating from within it. And the sooner it is out of your life, the better off you are likely to be.

Regardless which stone or stones you may find yourself drawn to, there are some very important things to remember: Do not underestimate the power of gemstones. Respect your personal stones as you would any other sacred ritual tool, and always pay heed to your sixth sense (or intuitive powers) when working with stones. Never question why a particular stone has entered your life. Instead, offer your thanks to Mother Nature or Goddess Earth for the magickal gift she has bestowed upon you. Always use it wisely and only for good, and it will become a special friend to you and serve you well for many years to come.

> *"Crystals are surely one of the most beautiful gifts from the earth, and a wonderful compliment to your altar and your magical work."*

> —Susan Bowes, *Notions and Potions*

Chapter 1

The Calling of the Stones

My attraction to gemstones and gem magick began as a teenager, with turquoise being the very first type of stone to which I felt strongly attuned. It was during a visit to a trading post on an Indian Reservation in the Southwest that this beautiful blue stone first "called" to me. I must admit that my knowledge concerning turquoise was rather limited at that time. I only knew that it was a sacred stone to many Native American tribes (including the Hopi, from which my paternal grandmother hailed) and that it was considered to be a stone associated with the month of December—the month in which I was born.

I had not been aware of its centuries-old reputation for attracting good luck, nor its amuletic use for warding off the evil eye. However, from the very moment that I tried on my first piece of turquoise jewelry, I instinctively knew this was a stone that possessed great energy and extremely good vibrations. To this day, whenever I wear a turquoise pendant or ring, or carry with me a small piece of turquoise in a mojo bag, I usually feel surrounded by a sense of serenity and protection.

The protective and good luck qualities of turquoise have demonstrated themselves to me on more than one occasion. For instance, the time when my man and I were traveling on a highway just outside of Philadelphia and the automobile ahead of us suddenly swerved out of its lane and collided with another vehicle. To my immediate horror, both cars began to spin out in our direction, and one came within an inch or so of the driver's side of our car. It all happened very fast, but we somehow managed to dodge the out-of-control vehicle just in the nick of time, being spared from what surely would have been a devastating, and perhaps fatal, accident. I often wonder if we would have been so fortunate had I not been wearing my protective turquoise pendant at the time.

Onyx—a mysterious-looking black stone believed in the Middle Ages to house a demon that provoked melancholy, nightmares, and quarrels between lovers—is another gemstone to which I am strongly drawn. (Coincidentally, it is a stone associated with Capricorn—the astrological sign under which I was born.) In spite of its unfavorable reputation from olden times, the onyx, like turquoise, actually possesses protective qualities and is employed by a number of Witches and other occult practitioners in rituals for magickal self-defense.

Onyx first came into my life a number of years ago when I resided in the quaint and historic country town of Fort Covington in northern Upstate New York, where I presided as High Priestess of Coven Mandragora. One evening an informal get-together of Pagans was held at my house and one of my guests (a young raven-haired Witch who was close friends with one of my fellow coven members) surprised me with a most exquisite present— an enchanting antique necklace of silver and onyx that had been in her family for several generations. It seemed to vibrate with what I can only describe as "dark goddess energy" and soon became the traditional ritual jewelry for me to wear whenever performing rituals that invoke Hecate or other goddesses belonging to the darker realms. (Please note: The terms "dark" and "darker realms" should not necessarily be equated with "black magick" or "evil." The Dark Goddess is the Crone aspect of the Triple Goddess, and, in most Wiccan circles, is symbolized by the new moon. She is a wise woman, warrioress, healer, seductress, destroyer, and keeper of magick and mystery.)

Because of its strong Saturn/Mars influence and probably also its black color, the onyx is often put to malevolent use by some practitioners who find this stone to be a highly effective tool for dispatching vengeance spells, curses, and the like. However, the onyx can also be made to work to protect an individual against negativity and evil intents, and even deflect them back upon their original senders.

The moonstone is another personal favorite of mine. It is a stone popular among a good number of Witches, not only for its opalescent beauty, but also for its strong connection with lunar magick and all goddesses who are associated with the moon and its psychic and feminine energies.

I often wear moonstone when using a dowsing pendulum, reading tarot cards, or scrying a crystal ball or the flickering flame of a candle. I find that it helps to raise my psychic sensitivity and puts me more in tune with the various tools of divination with which I work. I have also found that, when crystal-gazing, the images I receive come to me faster and are enhanced in clarity if I encircle the crystal ball with seven small moonstones. (In numerology, seven is the number associated with things of a psychic nature.)

Moonstone is also a beneficial stone to have if you are experiencing difficulty sleeping. Before bedtime, drink a warm cup of chamomile or valerian tea and place a moonstone underneath your pillow. In most cases, this should work to bring you a restful night's sleep.

Some people have asked me if it is all right to wear or carry different types of stones at the same time, fearing that their different energies may somehow clash. Unless I am working a spell that calls for the energies of a specific gemstone, I will sometimes wear a combination of different gemstones if they are aesthetically pleasing to me and if the combination feels right. If, for some reason, it does not, then I listen to what my feelings tell me. In my opinion, that is really the best way to make a determination, for it is through our emotions, thoughts, and intuitions that the mysterious energies contained within stones subtly communicate with us.

Lee Prosser is a Shaman friend of mine who shares my interest in the occult lore and application of stones. Like many other magickally inclined individuals, he felt the calling of the stones at a young age. In the following essay titled "Witch Stones," Lee shares some of his thoughts and experiences concerning various stones.

Witch Stones
by Lee Prosser

When I was a child, I went to family picnics and outings, and I recall how my Uncle Willard took me on rock-hunting expeditions. He made every rock or fossil come alive with his stories. I recall him telling me once: "Every stone has a special story. Every stone will share its story with you. If you feel attracted to a stone, it is the stone calling to you in friendship. Pick it up, look it over, and feel its surface. What is it trying to tell you? Listen with your heart." As a result of this advice, I have collected stones all of my life, and each had something to share with me! My experiences have always been positive ones on my rock-hunting expeditions throughout the years, and that also includes collecting shells on beaches. I am grateful to my Uncle Willard for awakening my interest in stones at an early age. I share my interest with those who are of like mind.

Being a proficient Witch or Shaman means having a proficient working knowledge of stones and the use of them. Stones in their individual ways are indeed blessed with spiritual power. The use of stones in religions is old, perhaps coming into use with the first ancients who sought to form spiritual and religious rituals, and if one reviews ancient religions, the use of stones in some form of expression becomes apparent. Stones are used in magick. Let me share a few of my favorite stones with you.

The moonstone has long been one of my favorite stones. It is most often associated with the Moon, the Element of Water, and all lunar goddesses, such as Isis and Diana. Its powers include love, divination, protection, youth, and sleep, among other attributes. It can be white, pink, or blue and is feldspar. Many writers have stated it is most powerful during the waxing moon. Moonstone is a receptive stone and will draw love into a person's life. Many people place a moonstone under their pillow at night for a restful sleep. I have found this to work, and also there are the dreams that can come while sleeping. It can be associated with gardening, and is a protective stone carried or worn as jewelry. The moonstone can help in developing psychic abilities such as foreseeing future events.

A good illustrated guide to rocks and minerals will help in identifying moonstone and others. One of the small, easily back-packed books I carry with me when rock hunting is Michael O'Donoghue's *The Pocket Guide to Rocks and Minerals*, which contains more than 270 color illustrations. In the wilds, this book comes in handy as a nice reference and identification tool.

Jade is another favorite of mine. Like moonstone, it speaks to me. A receptive stone, it is associated with the planet Venus, the Element of Water, and the deities Buddha and Maat. Its powers are great, and, depending upon which of the many sources you come across, those powers will usually include protection, wisdom, healing, love, and prosperity. It is oftentimes used in magickal rituals for healing and to draw love. It is believed to be helpful in healing the heart and kidneys, and some writers also add healing of stomach complaints. According to the ancients, jade is carried or worn to receive wisdom and sound reasoning. Many Witches are known to wear jade during magick rituals that require self-defense against some evil force. Jade is also worn and carried for good health.

Turquoise is another wonderful stone to have near you. While I was living in New Mexico, it was possible to find much quality turquoise. Although I still live in the Southwest, but not in New Mexico, I still dream of the New Mexico areas where I located a wide range of stones. A receptive stone, associated with the planets Venus and Neptune, and with Earth as an Element, turquoise is greatly associated with American Indian beliefs and the ancient Egyptian deity named Hathor. Some sources list Buddha as another associated deity. Its powers include friendship, luck, healing, love, and protection, to list but a few.

Many people wear a turquoise ring to protect themselves from evil and accidents. Used in love rituals, it is also used to attract good health and heal the body and mind. The blue color of turquoise is relaxing to meditate upon, and the stone is carried to bring good luck.

Amethyst is a receptive stone associated with the planets Neptune and Jupiter, and the Element of Water. Bacchus and Diana are among the deities associated with it. Amethyst, a deep purple to pale lavender variety of quartz, is a powerful spiritual stone. It is reputed to be effective in increasing psychic awareness and divinatory skills. Some writers believe that when this stone is held in the right hand during a court case or lawsuit, it will bring good fortune and an honest verdict to the holder of the stone.

I carry a small sample of each stone in my wallet. Four small pebbles, so to speak, wrapped within a folded piece of white paper that has the images of goddesses Bast and Durga hand drawn upon it. On that paper is written something my late Uncle Willard told me: "Remember a stone is what you make of it. If you are hurting in some way, walk along and a stone will come to you. Tell it your hurt and then throw it away, far from you. The hurt will be gone. The stone will destroy the hurt and return to its normal state, ready to help again."

A very ancient spell for stones, still in use today and prevalent in the Southwestern United States, is to find a stone and place it in your throwing hand. Consider what you want to banish from your life, consider it clearly and in detail so that the stone knows truly what is in your heart, then throw it as far away from you as possible, saying, "I am free, I am free, I am free."

I recall Uncle Willard sharing with me his knowledge of the bloodstone, which has a long history in matters of the occult—a history that is both fascinating and enduring. The bloodstone is a green chalcedony, and it is flecked with beautiful red spots that come alive with movement the longer you stare upon them. The red spots are like little living flames of fire, burning bright. Bloodstone had its place in the lore of ancient Egypt for many purposes, such as opening locked doors. This stone is used for attracting wealth and success in winning legal matters, and also lengthening the life span of the one who carries it. Many people carry a bloodstone to ensure good health and keep the blood healthy.

Sitting atop my desk is a hand-sized hunk of meteorite that was given to me by a very interesting individual of Spanish heritage while I was living in Roswell, New Mexico. It is deep black in color and extremely cold to the touch, but the energy is there when I hold it in my hand. Roswell, New Mexico has many meteorites in its area. This is one of the more beautiful and powerful ones that I have seen.

Actually a metal, the meteorite has long been held in reverence by many cultures, and is noted for its protection and astral projection powers. Associated with the Great Mother deity and the Element of Fire, it is considered to possess a projective energy and is also known by the name of aerolith. A small fragment of meteorite can be held in the hand to aid meditation, or placed under the pillow during sleep to achieve astral projection. It can also be placed on the altar for protection.

I remember one sweet, warm summer day in the hill country of Southwestern Missouri. I was 16 years old and magick was everywhere in those timeless hills. My Uncle Willard and I were roaming the rocky beach near the river and we discovered thousands of baseball-sized geodes in the area, both on land and in the water.

Geodes are also known by their folk names of echites, eagle stones, and rock eggs. Their powers are associated with childbirth and fertility, and meditation. For meditation purposes, the geode can be held in the hand or placed on the altar. Geodes are geologically explained as hollow concretions containing crystals. The inside of the geode is usually amethyst or quartz crystal.

I recall seeing one geode which had been cut in half, and it was a beautiful amethyst, the inside looking like a beautiful collection of melted candles. I think of the inside of a geode and the image of melted candles in the form of stone comes to mind. Uncle Willard and I had collected a dozen of the geodes that were whole, and about 10 that had been broken open. I remember Uncle Willard handing me a quartz geode that was cracked open, exposing the interior. He handed the stone to me and said: "On the outside, a rough rock. On the inside, there is beauty. The strength is always within. The strength within is what makes everything else work. People have the same strength within, and all they have to do is wake up and look within. When you can look within, you realize you are connected to everything. There is a oneness there that is universal. When you are one with that, your power is tremendous. You can do anything! You can create anything you set your mind to create! You are one with all, and all is one with you."

Hematite is one of the most unusual of stones. Noted for its healing and divination powers, it has a silvery black color and has among its folk titles such names as cats paw, volcano spit, volcano tear, and silver fire. It has a highly projective base and its natural Element is Fire. Use of hematite for divination purposes has produced valid results as claimed by many people, and I am among them.

Hematite is also considered by many sources to be a grounding stone and one capable of removing illness from the body. Whether used in visualization, worn as a ring or a necklace, or placed directly on an injured area of the body, the hematite is reputed to hasten the recovery and healing process, and some sources have claimed that its powers help eliminate back pain and joint pain. Some people also use it on their animal companions to insure their recovery and well being. I oftentimes wear a hematite ring on my finger because it is a remarkable healing stone that has a special feel to it. With its background clouded in mystery, hematite remains one of the most useful, yet unknown, stones in the world. There are many secrets to be discovered about hematite.

One time I was walking along the beach in Santa Monica, California, with my friend, writer Christopher Isherwood. He came across a holey stone, picked it up, examined it, and gave it to me as a gift. It was a round, light-colored rock about two inches in diameter, with an off-center quarter-inch hole in the center. Holey stones come in different shapes and are believed to bring protection and health to the person who has one.

In December of 1968 I visited novelist/composer Paul Bowles at his hotel in Santa Monica, and he gave me one of several holey stones that he, too, had picked up on the beach. It was a small blue specimen with two holes. Bowles was a keen observer interested in Witchcraft and the supernatural, which was reflected at times in his fiction. He was also the godfather to my daughters.

I still have the two holey stones given to me by Isherwood and Bowles. They are tied together with a blue ribbon, and simply by holding them can I recall vividly how they were given to me.

Over the years I have been given various stones by friends and relatives, including my Uncle Willard, my mother, my children, and my late grandmother, Archie T. Firestone, who gave me a small red ruby and told me it would bring me luck. Different stones from different places with different stories hold special memories for me!

I once came across a large rock that was shaped like a face, complete with eyes, nose, and mouth, as a result of water erosion and the passage of time. I have kept it safely wrapped in white felt, taken it out when its presence was needed, and replaced it safely afterwards in a small wooden box. Over the years I grew fond of the stone, and one time, during a Shamanic journey, it told me that its name was Hank. I believe this unusual stone holds special powers that are telepathic links to other times, and with the proper setting for meditation and relaxation, it can help one to explore other dimensions concerning past life situations. Sometimes Hank is feminine, and at other times Hank is masculine.

Stones are important in the life of the individual. They have spiritual and magickal powers. They are of the earth, and their positive nature will help eliminate the negative forces that attempt to come into our lives. They benefit those who use them properly in achieving personal goals.

Witch stones are a natural part of existence. Witch stones are a blessing to those who know them. All we have to do is pause long enough to hear them call out to our minds and say our names, and we have a friend from nature.

Witchcraft is a positive and compassionate Earth-oriented religion, and gemstones are a part of its heritage. To be an honest Witch is to understand that which has been around each of us since the beginning of time and to use that knowledge for the benefit of oneself and for helping others in a positive manner.

Lee Prosser was born on December 31, 1944 in Missouri and has written more than 2,000 published works. He follows an eclectic path, and has held a lifelong interest in Witchcraft, Shamanism, and Vedanta. His most recent book publications include a published memoir, Isherwood, Bowles, Vedanta, Wicca, and Me, *and a published collection of essays and other writings titled* Night Tigers. *Lee Prosser's interests include exploring ghost towns, photography, cats, painting oils and watercolors, composing music, and collecting postcards. He lives in the Southwestern United States.*

Chapter 2

Preparations and Intentions

Before using any stone or crystal as a tool to create magick or to heal those afflicted by pain and illness, it is vital that it be ritually cleansed (or cleared) and then charged. Cleansing a stone or crystal removes negative vibrations from it without affecting its magickal properties. Charging it programs it with energy.

Cleansing

There are many different methods for cleansing a crystal, but the most popular ones include:

- ☆ Soaking it in saltwater or sea water for at least 24 hours.
- ☆ Holding it (with its termination pointing downward) under cold running tap water for at least one minute.
- ☆ Placing it outdoors in direct sunlight from 10 a.m. to 2 p.m.
- ☆ Burying it in the earth for at least seven days.
- ☆ Covering it with sea salt for one to seven days.

☆ Visualizing it surrounded by a white or golden light beaming from your Third Eye chakra.

☆ Stroking it with a tape demagnetizer.

☆ Soaking it in sage tea.

☆ Exhaling upon it.

☆ Petitioning a deity to purify and bless it.

Smudging (a purification method used for centuries by American Indian medicine men, African witch doctors, and other Shamans) is another popular method for ridding crystals and stones of stored-up negativity. In this method, incense or a small bundle of dried herbs is burned, and the crystal is then passed through the fragrant smoke several times, while an affirmation that it is being purified is stated. Cedar, sage, and sweetgrass are the three plants most commonly used for smudging and eliminating negativity.

The method of cleansing that one uses is entirely a matter of personal choice, and one based on his or her magickal tradition, spiritual beliefs, and perceptions of energy. If you are unsure which cleansing method is best for your crystal or stone, allow your own intuition to be your guide or consult an oracle such as a pendulum.

The amount of time required for cleansing a crystal or stone depends on the amount of negative energy buildup that needs to be cleared from it. A small amount of negativity may take anywhere from a few minutes to a few hours to clear, while a large amount may require several days to a week or longer.

Some persons who are new to gemstone sorcery may be wondering how one determines when a stone needs cleansing. The answer to this is simple: When you start to sense a decrease in a stone's magickal or healing energy, or when it begins to feel sticky when you touch it, this is a sign that a cleansing is in order.

A stone that has absorbed a great deal of negativity over a period of time will also give off negative vibrations, which can be felt as either a subtle or intense negative energy current by those who possess a higher level of psychic sensitivity than the average person. Individuals who are gifted with the ability to read auras will sometimes perceive it as a black or dark-colored mist or halo emanating from the crystal or stone.

If you do healing work with crystals and gemstones or have them on display in your home and find yourself frequently experiencing headaches, depression, feelings of inertia, and/or unexplained physical illnesses, this may be a warning sign that your stones are giving off negative vibrations and need to be cleansed.

After the stone has been ritually cleansed, take it and hold it in your receptive hand (the left if you're right-handed, and the right if you're left-handed). If its energy vibrations feel normal to you, this indicates that the cleansing has been met by success. (The more you work with stones, the more familiar you will become with their different energies.) But if you perceive the energy to be unhealthy, disturbing in any way, or just "not right," then the stone's cleansing process will need to be extended for a longer period of time.

A ritual cleansing should always be done when acquiring a new crystal or stone to remove any past influences from it. Those that are used for healing work should be thoroughly cleansed before each and every use and after being handled by persons other than the healer to whose energies the stones are attuned.

Stones that have been used for negative magick (such as hexing or the conjuring of evil entities) should never be employed for any type of positive spellwork (especially rituals that involve healing), unless they are thoroughly cleansed beforehand. To use such a stone without first cleansing it would be a terribly unwise thing to do. Its negative vibrations would likely interfere with the energy of your spell, neutralizing or possibly even reversing its positive effects.

Charging

Charging a crystal or stone is relatively simple and can be accomplished in the following manner: On the first night of the full moon (when lunar energies are at their peak), take the crystal you wish to charge and place it in your power hand. (This is the hand with which you normally use to write.) As you hold it, visualize your specific need or desire, and will your energy to flow from your hand into the crystal. Continue doing this until you feel that the crystal is attuned to your energies and vibrating with your personal power.

Repeat the charging process prior to each spell or ritual you perform and you will find that the effects of your gemstone sorceries will be greatly enhanced.

Creating a Stone Altar

A stone altar is a Witch's center of power, meditation, and worship. One of its main functions is to hold ritual tools (such as athames, pentacles, chalices, bells, candles, books of shadows, wands, incense burners, and representations of particular gods and/or goddesses). Another is to provide a sacred place at which magickal rites and religious ceremonies can be carried out. It is, however, never used in Neo-Pagan Witchcraft for the purpose of human or animal sacrifice.

To create a simple stone altar, you will need two long stones of equal size and shape to serve as the base of the altar. It is important that the tops of both stones are smooth and level. You will also need a long flat stone to rest on top of the two base stones and serve as the top of the altar.

A stone altar can also be created by placing a large slab of marble or some other stone upon any small table or cabinet, or even the stump of a tree, as long as the top of it is level and flat. There are many other ways in which to make a stone altar, and the ones mentioned here are but a few ideas.

Some magickal practitioners are moved to engrave or paint runic names or magickal symbols on their stone altars, while others prefer a more plain appearance. How elaborate or how simple you make your stone altar depends entirely upon you and your personal needs and preferences.

A stone altar is suitable for all types of spellwork, religious ceremonies, and meditative rituals. It can be erected either indoors or outside, in a natural setting, and utilized by both solitaries and covens, regardless of tradition.

Deep in the forest behind my century-old Victorian house in Upstate New York was an unusual large rock formation that looked to be shrouded in mystery and enchantment. From it emanated a subtle energy that I, being a psychic-sensitive Witch, was able to immediately detect. On one side of the rock formation jutted an interesting stone ledge of several feet in length that made for an exquisite natural altar. Upon this wondrous gift from the Earth Mother, I performed many rituals of the olden ways, and I found that the stones, along with the trees of the forest, seemed to intensify the magickal energy that I raised.

I've always found outdoor rituals to be far more exhilarating than those performed within the confines of a man-made structure, and, because of this, the rock formation became an important part of my spiritual and magickal practices. The clearing where it stood was also a place of peace and solitude to where I frequently journeyed for meditation and to write, often being accompanied by my faithful cats.

A Wiccan Stone Altar

To create a stone altar for Wiccan rites, place a crystal sphere or any round holed stone to the left of the altar to symbolize the Goddess. Place a quartz crystal point or any phallic-shaped stone to the left of the altar to symbolize Her consort, the Horned God. Position a red candle between the two deity symbols to represent the divine energy of the Goddess and the God, as well as the ancient Element of Fire. (In place of the red candle, some Pagans prefer to work with white altar candles, while others like to incorporate candles bearing the color that corresponds to the deity or deities of their particular traditions. The decision whether to use white or colored candles on one's altar to represent a deity is, like so many facets of Pagan spirituality and folk magick, a matter of personal choice.)

Place a flat stone before the red candle to serve as an "offering stone." This can be used to receive offerings such as herbs, gemstones, cakes, flowers, fruit, wine, or honey. Place a small flat stone to the right of the offering stone to serve as a salt holder and to represent the ancient Element of Earth. To the left of the offering stone, place a concave stone (or seashell) and fill it with water to represent the ancient Element of Water. Incense is often used by Wiccans to represent the ancient Element of Air, and can be burned atop a flat stone placed before the offering stone.

For other ritual tools, there are various stone alternatives that can be used if you so desire. Using a flint or obsidian arrowhead as an athame and a long, thin terminated quartz crystal as a wand are but two examples.

To dedicate the stone altar to a particular Pagan deity, place between two altar candles in the center of the altar any stone (or number of stones) that corresponds to your god or goddess. For instance, a moonstone for Diana, Artemis, Selene, Isis, and all deities connected with the moon; a lava rock for Pele; a cat's eye for Bast; and so forth. For a list of other Pagan deities and their corresponding gemstones, see Appendix C: *Pagan Gods* and Appendix D: *Pagan Goddesses*.

A Triple Goddess Stone Altar

To dedicate a stone altar to the Triple Goddess, place a white candle affixed with a white gemstone (such as an opal or moonstone) at the left side of the altar to represent the Goddess in Her aspect of the Maiden. At the center of the altar, place a red candle affixed with a red gemstone (such as a ruby or garnet) to represent the Goddess in Her aspect of the Mother. At the right side of the altar, place a black candle affixed with a black gemstone (such as an onyx or obsidian) to represent the Goddess in Her aspect of the Crone.

Gemstones and the Four Cardinal Points

In addition to representing deities and the four ancient Elements, crystals and gemstones can be used to represent the four cardinal points, and placed at either the four sides of the altar or at the Watchtowers (the four directional points at the perimeter of a magick circle, also known as the *Directions* or the *Quarters*).

The ancient Mayans linked the direction of East with the metal gold, the direction of South with pearls, the direction of West with jade and turquoise, and the direction of North with bloodstone.

Use gemstones ruled by the Element of Air to represent the East; the Element of Fire to represent the South; the Element of Water to represent the West; and the Element of Earth to represent the North.

In addition, gemstones that match the colors corresponding to the cardinal points can be used. For instance: yellow or white stones for the East; red or orange stones for the South; blue or purple stones for the West; and green, black, or brown stones for the North. However, not all traditions ascribe the same colors to the four cardinal points. (If in doubt, follow your own intuition and do what feels correct and works best for you.)

Homemade Spells and Magickal Intentions

Many modern Witches (myself included) prefer working with their own customized homemade spells as opposed to following those in books written by others.

There is absolutely nothing wrong with a Witch creating his or her own spells. In many cases it actually serves to make the magick all the more stronger. However, to ensure successful spellcasting, certain age-old occult guidelines must be adhered to, such as working in harmony with the energy of the lunar phases (waxing to increase or attract, waning to decrease or repel), the four Elements, planetary hours, and so forth.

For those desiring to create their own gemstone spells and talismans, the following alphabetically arranged list categorizes popular precious and semiprecious stones by their magickal intentions, for easy reference.

Anaphrodisiac (Opposite of Aphrodisiac): Onyx.

Aphrodisiac: Pearl.

Animals: Boulder matrix opal (to access one's animal guides), cat's eye (for all spellwork relating to cats), cylindrite, faustite, ganophyllite, horneblende (for communicating with the physical and spiritual animal worlds), stibnite (a totem stone for the wolf), and tiger's eye.

Astral Projection/Astral Travel: Agate (Brazilian), alexandrite, ametrine, angelite, apophyllite, astrophyllite, azulicite, benitoite, calcite, caledonite, celestite, florencite, geode, iolite, jasper, kyanite, lepidocrocite, lepidolite, linarite, lodestone, milarite, mohawkite, obsidian (blue or electric-blue sheen), petalite, quartz crystal (especially double terminated and quartz penetrated by black tourmaline crystals), ramsdellite, richterite, rutile, sapphire (blue), spinel (dark blue), tellurium, tephroite, tunnellite (to strengthen the silver cord), and turquoise.

Banishing Evil Spirits: Diamond, emerald, jasper, and jet.

Bravery: Agate (tawny), amethyst, aquamarine, beryl, bloodstone, carnelian, diamond, garnet, lapis lazuli, sard, sardonyx, tiger's eye, tourmaline (red), and turquoise.

Clairvoyance: See *Psychic Powers.*

Divination: Azurite, emerald, flint, hematite, jet, lamprophyllite, mica, moonstone, mosandrite, obsidian, opal, palermoite (stimulates the ability for palmistry), sapphire, and tiger's eye.

Dreams: Amethyst, augelite, azurite, beta quartz, Chinese writing rock, dickite, garnet, jade, jasper (red), kyanite, lapis lazuli, manganosite, moonstone, opal, peridot, quartz crystal, rhonite, ruby, sapphire (green), and tourmaline (blue). See also *Prophetic Dreams.*

Emotional Balance: Carnelian, emerald, magnetite, ruby, sapphire, sardonyx, topaz, and turquoise.

Exorcism: Bloodstone, flint, garnet, jasper (red), lava rock, onyx, pipestone, rhodocrosite, rhodonite, ruby, sard, sardonyx, and tourmaline (red and watermelon). See also *Ghosts/ Spirits.*

Fairy Magick: Cross stone (a form of andalusite), flint (also known as elf-arrow, elf-shot, and fairy-shot, and once used by the Irish to ward off mischievous fairy-folk), holey stones (to see fairies), and staurolite (also known as fairy-cross, fairy-stone, and fairy-tears).

Fertility: Agate (green), amber, geodes, jade, manganite, moonstone, pearl, quartz crystal (pink or rose), sonolite, and tourmaline (orange).

Gambling: Amazonite, aventurine, and cat's eye.

Garden Magick: Agate (moss), jade, and moonstone.

Ghosts/Spirits: Amber (to repel), amethyst (to conjure), carnelian with chlorite and ruby (to banish), cat's eye chrysoberyl (to conjure good spirits, repel evil spirits), chrysolite (to repel) green jasper (to repel), peridot (used by the ancient Romans to repel ghosts), quartz crystal (to conjure and communicate with spirits, especially when used in the form of a pendulum), sapphire (to conjure), and zircon (to repel). See also *Exorcism*.

Good Luck: Alexandrite, amber, Apache tear, aventurine, chalcedony, chrysoprase, cross stone, jade, jet, lepidolite, moonstone, olivine, opal (black), pearl, ruby, sardonyx, tiger's eye, topaz, and turquoise.

Grounding: Calcite (pink), hematite, jasper (brown), kunzite, moonstone, obsidian, petalite, smoky quartz, tourmaline (black), and zircon (brown, also known as malacon).

Healing: See "Ailments and Gemstones" (pages 92–98) and "Amuletic Gemstones" (pages 61–87).

Insight: Agate (green), obsidian, sapphire, and sardonyx.

Invisibility: Bloodstone, cat's eye (to make warriors invisible in battle, according to Arab legend), onyx, opal, sapphire, sardonyx, and topaz.

Justice: Bloodstone, hessonite, jadeite (black), jasper (red), jet, obsidian, onyx, serpentine, tourmaline (black), and zircon (hyacinth).

Love Magick: Agate, alexandrite, amber, amethyst, beryl, calcite, chrysocolla, emerald, jade, lapis lazuli, lepidolite, lodestone, magnetite, malachite, moonstone, olivine, pearl, rhodocrosite, rose quartz, sapphire, sard, topaz, tourmaline (pink), and turquoise.

Magickal Power (to Increase): Amber, bloodstone, calcite, magnetite, malachite, opal, quartz crystal, and ruby.

Magickal Self-defense: Bloodstone, garnet, jade, jasper (red), lava rock, onyx, pipestone, rhodocrosite, rhodonite, ruby, sard, sardonyx, sapphire, and tourmaline (red).

Mental Clarity: Amber, amethyst, beryl, chalcedony, fluorite, jacinth, moonstone, obsidian, ruby, and sardonyx.

Money, Prosperity, Wealth: Aventurine, bloodstone, calcite, cat's eye, chrysoprase, emerald, jade, mother-of-pearl, olivine, opal, pearl, peridot, ruby, sapphire, spinel, staurolite, tiger's eye, topaz, tourmaline (green), and zircon.

Necromancy: Sapphire.

Nightmares (to Prevent): Chalcedony, citrine, coral, garnet, jet, lepidolite, and ruby.

Persuasion Over Others: Apache tear, hematite, jasper (brown), jet, obsidian, onyx, serpentine, and tourmaline (black).

Prophetic Dreams: Aquamarine, beryl, chalcedony, moonstone, mother-of-pearl, pearl, quartz crystal, sapphire, and selenite.

Protection: Agate, amber, Apache tear, beryl, calcite, carnelian, cat's eye (especially against the evil eye), chalcedony, chrysoprase, citrine, coral, diamond, emerald, garnet, jade, jasper, jet, lapis lazuli, lepidolite, magnetite, malachite, marble, mica, moonstone, mother-of-pearl, obsidian, olivine, onyx (against the evil eye), pearl, peridot, pumice, quartz crystal, ruby, sapphire (against the evil eye), sard, sardonyx, serpentine, staurolite, sunstone, tiger's eye, topaz, tourmaline (black), tourmaline (red), turquoise, zircon (clear), and zircon (red).

Psychic Attack (to Ward Off): Aegirine, agate, asbestos (historically regarded as a magickal stone by the ancients, but now known to be unsafe to handle due to health concerns), betafite, carnelian (with chlorite and ruby crystals), carrollite, cat's eye, chalcedony, chrysoprase, coral, garnet, jade, jet, lava rock, limonite, moonstone, obsidian, onyx, peridot, ruby, sapphire, sard, staurolite, sunstone, tiger's eye, topaz, tourmaline (black), and turquoise.

Psychic Powers (to Awaken or Strengthen): Agate (rose-eye) amethyst, apatite, aquamarine, azurite, beryl, bloodstone, cherry opal, citrine, emerald, jet, lapis lazuli, lavender quartz, lepidolite, mica, moonstone, obsidian (purple), opal, petalite, quartz crystal, sapphire, smithsonite, and sugilite.

Strength (Physical): Agate, amber, beryl, bloodstone, diamond, garnet, jasper (red), onyx, pipestone, ruby, sard, sardonyx, and tourmaline (red).

Success in Business: Amber, bloodstone, calcite (orange), diamond, malachite, pipestone, sunstone, tiger's eye, topaz, tourmaline (green), and zircon (yellow).

Travel (Safety During): Amethyst, chalcedony, hyacinth, jacinth, and zircon (orange).

Weatherworking: Agate (moss), beryl, bloodstone (to cause thunder, lightning, and tempest), dicinite, fulgurite, jade (to bring rain), jasper (green), pitchstone (to bring rain), quartz crystal (to bring rain), turquoise, and wilkeite.

Wisdom: Agate, aventurine, chrysocolla, coral, jade, jasper (mottled), mica, pumice, sapphire, sodalite, and sugilite.

Chapter 3

Spells, Rituals, and Charms

agick, according to occultist Aleister Crowley, is "the science and art of causing change to occur in conformity to the will." It has been practiced in various forms since prehistoric times and by every culture. The ancient civilizations of Mesopotamia and the Mediterranean are known to have practiced the magickal arts quite extensively.

The simplest form of magick is the spell (also known as *mechanical sorcery*), which is basically the performance of a physical act, often accompanied by the recitation of a magickal incantation, to achieve a particular result. Spells that involve petitioning the aid of a deity, demon, angel, or spirit, are considered to be a higher form of sorcery.

One of the secrets to casting successful spells lies in the act of visualizing one's intent during the spellcasting process. Using your mind's eye to see your goals as being already achieved or the object of your heart's desire as being already obtained is essential to the magickal manifestation of your wishes.

The raising of power is equally as important as visualization when it comes to the casting of spells, and this can be accomplished through various means. Chanting, dancing, scourging, and sex magick (sexual intercourse or erotic self-stimulation) are among the most popular power-building methods used by various traditions. At the point when the power reaches its peak, the spellcaster then releases it and directs it toward his or her goal.

In most cases, working in harmony with lunar phases, planetary hours, and astrological influences, in conjunction with visualization and energy-raising techniques, will lend greater power to one's spellwork, whether it be of a so-called white, black, or gray nature.

In addition, many Witches and magicians feel that keeping their spells secret until they come to fruition will prevent them from losing their potency. To speak about a spell before it is cast or while it is in progress is a sure way to jinx it, and the old expression, "magick spoken is magick lost," reflects this line of thought.

"The success of a spell rests on the power and will raised and the skill with which they are focused and projected."

—Rosemary Ellen Guiley

Male and Female Energy Stones

The following stones are said to vibrate with male (also known as projective) energy, and are magickally appropriate for spells and rituals that repel, as well as for workings that involve God energy, males and masculinity, virility, power, success, exorcism, protection, and things of a physical or intellectual nature:

Agate (banded, black, brown, or red), amber, Apache tear, aventurine, bloodstone, calcite (orange), carnelian, cat's eye, citrine, diamond, flint, fluorite, garnet, hematite, jasper (mottled or red), lava rock, mica, obsidian, onyx, opal (black or fire), pipestone, pumice, quartz crystal (rutilated or tourmalated), rhodocrosite, rhodonite, ruby, sard, sardonyx, serpentine, sphene, spinel, sunstone, tiger's eye, topaz, tourmaline (red), and zircon.

The following gemstones are said to vibrate with female (also known as receptive) energy. They are magickally appropriate for spells and rituals that attract, as well as for workings that involve Goddess energy, females and femininity, fertility, growth, nurturing, and things of an emotional, spiritual, or psychic nature:

Agate (blue lace, green, or moss), amethyst, aquamarine, azurite, beryl, calcite (blue, green, or pink), celestite, chalcedony, chrysocolla, chrysoprase, coral, emerald, jade, jasper (brown or green), jet, kunzite, lapis lazuli, malachite, marble, moonstone, mother-of-pearl, olivine, opal, pearl, peridot, quartz crystal (blue, green, rose, or smoky), sapphire, selenite, sodalite, sugilite, tourmaline (black, blue, green, or pink), and turquoise.

The Magick of Wands

The wand is a powerful tool of magick, said to date back to prehistoric times. It is employed by Witches and magicians mainly for directing magickal energy during spells and rituals, but can also be used to cast circles, enhance one's focus, invoke spirits, heal the sick, charge objects and water, and so forth. The wand is also used in rituals to represent the ancient Element of Fire or Air, depending on which Pagan tradition one follows.

Elder, rowan, willow, hazel, and hawthorn are the types of wood traditionally used by European Witches in the making of wands. Metals can also be used for wand-making, and the most popular of these are: silver (ruled by the Moon and the Element of Water), copper (ruled by the planet Venus and the Element of Water), brass (ruled by the Sun and the Element of Fire), and gold (ruled by the Sun and the Element of Fire).

Wands of silver or copper possess receptive (also known as feminine) energy, while those of brass or gold possess energy that is projective (also known as masculine).

In modern times it is not unusual for wooden or metal wands to have affixed to one or both ends a quartz crystal, a faceted gem, or a polished stone for the amplification of magickal energies. And there are even some wands made entirely out of crystal.

Most Witches feel that crafting your own wand (and other rituals tools, if at all possible) is far better than purchasing a ready-made one from a store because when you make it yourself, you put your unique personal energies and intentions into it. And by personalizing it in this way, the magick that you create with it will be all the more powerful. Making a wand is not really that difficult of a project—directions follow for making one.

Directions for Making a Copper and Crystal Wand

To make your own wand, take a hollow copper tube (eight to 12 inches in length) and affix a quartz crystal to one of its ends with the aid of a hot glue gun. If you desire, you may place magickal herbs, small gemstones, amulets, talismans, or rolled-up pieces of parchments containing written spells inside the copper tube before sealing the other end. Use the hot glue gun to affix a copper cap, a quartz crystal, a small crystal ball, or a gemstone to the other end of the copper tube, and you now have a basic copper and crystal wand.

You can cover the copper with leather or cloth and/or glue smaller crystals and stones, feathers, seashells, beads, and so forth to it. You can also inscribe or paint runes, magickal sigils, or your personal astrological symbols upon the wand to further personalize it. The possibilities are endless, limited only by the power of your imagination. Be creative, but do bear in mind that a small simple wand works just as effectively as a large and elaborately decorated one. It is not the size, expense, or fanciness that gives a wand its power—it is the amount of energy that you direct into it when you create and work with it that empowers it.

After creating your wand, consecrate it and then charge it with intention. Keep it on your altar and do not let anyone else handle or use it, otherwise it will absorb their energies and you will have to reconsecrate and recharge it.

Talismanic Rings

The crafting and wearing of talismanic rings date back to medieval times and was an art employed for a variety of purposes, including the healing of physical ailments, the sending and lifting of curses, divination, the casting of amatory enchantments, and the evoking and banishing of spirits, elementals, angels, and demons.

Ceremonial magicians of old believed that for any talisman to effectively attract the influences of a certain planet, it had to be fashioned from a material ruled by that planet. According to Richard Cavendish, in his classic book *The Black Arts*, this needed to be done "at a time when the planet is radiating its influence with maximum power, when it is in the ascendant or at mid-sky or well aspected or in an appropriate zodiac sign."

The following chart contains a list of heavenly bodies and the materials that have historically been made into talismanic rings intended to attract their influences.

Body	Attributes	Talismanic Materials
Sun	Achievement of goals, success, purification, the overcoming of obstacles, and divination.	Ring should be made of gold and set with a stone of either diamond or topaz.
Moon	Growth, protection, emotional healing, nurturing, reconciliation, children, voyages, and anything related to water.	Ring should be made of silver and set with a stone of pearl, crystal, or quartz.
Mars	Passion, bravery, protection, competition, discord, bloodletting, and anything related to war.	Ring should be made of iron and set with a stone of ruby or any other red-colored gem.
Mercury	Communication, science, writing, clairvoyance, divination, and apparitions.	Ring should be made of mercury (quicksilver) and set with a stone of opal or agate. *Warning: It is poisonous to touch, breathe, or ingest mercury. Aluminum is a safer Mercury-ruled metal to use, despite the fact that it is a modern metal with no magickal history.*
Jupiter	Physical healing, protection, money, and friendship.	Ring should be made of tin and set with a stone of amethyst, carnelian, or sapphire.
Venus	Love, fertility, physical beauty, and traveling.	Ring should be made of copper and set with a stone of emerald or turquoise.
Saturn	Controlling, cursing, binding, separation, hedonism, money, and all things related to death. *Note: Using magick to curse or control the free will of others has, for centuries, been an accepted practice among some practitioners of Sorcery and Witchcraft. However, it is generally frowned upon by most Neo-Pagans and is in no way advocated by the publisher of this book.*	Ring should be made of lead and set with a stone of onyx or sapphire. *Warning: Lead is toxic when absorbed by the body. Therefore, a safer Saturn-ruled metal to use would be pewter.*

The Evil Eye

Since ancient times, various gemstones, both precious and semiprecious, have been employed the world over as amulets to protect against those who were believed to possess the malevolent powers of the evil eye.

According to E. A. Wallis Budge's *Amulets and Superstitions*, the following stones are prized for their alleged ability to ward off the evil eye: agate (popular among Italians and Persians), alum (popular in Africa), amber (in the shape of a phallus), asbestos (unsafe to handle, but used historically), asphalt (in the shape of a cross), bloodstone, carbuncle, carnelian, chalcedony, coral, crystal, diamond, emerald, hematite, jasper, jet (popular in Egypt, India, and Italy), malachite, milkstone (galaktite), onyx (popular in India and Persia), opal, peridot (when worn on the left arm), sapphire, and turquoise (popular in the Orient).

Protection Against Black Magick

To magickally protect yourself against all forms of black magick, wear a turquoise stone (preferably in the shape of a horse or a sheep) as an amulet. To keep its power strong, anoint it every Thursday at sunrise with a drop of "protection" oil (available in most occult shops).

Another powerful and ancient method of protection is to carry a piece of coral engraved with the following magickal square:

4	14	15	1
9	7	6	12
5	11	10	8
16	2	3	13

This magick square is known as the "Jupiter Magick Square," and is a variation of the magick square found in a copper engraving *(Melancholia I)* by a German Renaissance artist, Albrecht Durer. Note that the four numbers in each horizontal, vertical, and diagonal row add up to 34—a number believed by many numerologists to represent "Natural Law" and great spirituality. Some occultists believe that the number 34 possesses the power to guard against evil because the word *devil* appears 34 times in the Bible.

Garden Protection Spell

To keep any type of garden (whether it be for flowers, herbs, or vegetables) safe from evil influences and harm, take four small jade dragons and charge them by holding them in your cupped hands and visualizing protective energy in the form of a red glowing aura radiating around each dragon. As you do this, state your intention:

> With magickal energy do I charge these
> dragons of jade so that they may work both
> day and night to protect my garden from evil
> and harm.

Continue the visualization until you feel a warm tingling sensation and sense that the dragons have been sufficiently charged.

When the moon is full and her rays are bright and shining down upon the land, bury one of the magickally empowered jade dragons at the East end of the garden, and say:

> Dragon of the East,
> Empowered by charm,
> Protect this garden
> From evil and harm.

Bury the second jade dragon at the South end of the garden, and say:

> *Dragon of the South,*
> *Empowered by charm,*
> *Protect this garden*
> *From evil and harm.*

Bury the third jade dragon at the West end of the garden, and say:

> *Dragon of the West,*
> *Empowered by charm,*
> *Protect this garden*
> *From evil and harm.*

Bury the last dragon at the North end of the garden, and say:

> *Dragon of the North,*
> *Empowered by charm,*
> *Protect this garden*
> *From evil and harm.*

To Deflect a Wicked Spell

If you feel certain that a negative spell has been cast over you, your family, your home, or your business, one method to break it is to take a piece of jet and grind it into a powder. (For maximum effectiveness, be sure to do this on a Saturday and/or during a planetary hour ruled by Saturn.) Sprinkle the powdered jet upon a hot charcoal block in an incense burner as you recite the following incantation:

> *Stone of Saturn,*
> *Keep me protected,*
> *Let all curses be deflected.*
> *Let no evil fall on me,*
> *This is my will, so mote it be!*

A Binding Spell

When all else fails, a spell to bind negative energy is often necessary to prevent an evil-natured person from continuing to inflicting intentional harm upon you through means that are either magickal or mundane. For maximum effectiveness, this type of spell should be performed on Saturdays and/or during a planetary hour ruled by Saturn.

To cast a binding spell, light the wick of a black candle and then, using dragon's blood ink, write on a 3-inch by 3-inch piece of parchment the name of the person at whom the spell is directed. Chant his or her name and wrap the parchment around a piece of black onyx, securing it with a length of black ribbon or yarn as you visualize yourself surrounded by a protective sphere of white light, through which no energy of evil intent can penetrate. Bury it in the ground, and, while visualizing the person whose negative energy you are binding, repeat the following incantation nine times:

This magickal binding is now cast,
And may its power be steadfast.
I reinforce it, three times three,
This is my will, so mote it be.

Demons Associated With Gemstones

The Goetic demons are 72 spirits that, according to tradition, were commanded by King Solomon to build his temple. They are said to have been made popular by Aleister Crowley in his work with the Golden Dawn, and an account of their powers and offices can be found in *The Goetia* (the first of four parts of the *Lemegeton*, or *Lesser Key of Solomon*—a medieval grimoire).

The following Goetic demons (with title and planetary influence) are said to be learned in the virtues of all precious stones, and, when requested to do so, will teach mortals how to use them to produce magick: *Bathin* (Duke, Venus); *Bifrous* (Earl); *Decarabia* (Marquis); *Foras* (President, Mercury); *Marax* (President/Earl, Mercury/Mars); *Naberius* (Marquis, Moon); and *Stolas* (Prince, Jupiter).

The demon known as *Furneus* (Marquis, Moon) is said to appear in the form of a sea monster with fiery eyes and scales made of precious stones.

Please note: Unless you are an experienced practitioner of the Goetic arts (the ritual evocation of demons), I do not recommend that you attempt to summon any of the Goetic demons for any reason. While not all demons are evil, many are quite powerful and some can pose a dangerous threat to the magician if he or she performs an evocation in an incorrect manner.

Ancient Invisibility Spell

It is written in ancient grimoires that a magician can attain invisibility by placing a sardonyx talisman under his tongue and willing himself to become invisible. To reverse the spell, the magician places the same talisman under his tongue and wills himself to become visible again.

To Prevent Nightmares

When charged and placed underneath your pillow, attached to a dream-catcher, or worn to bed, any of the following stones will work well to keep your sleep free from unpleasant dreams: amethyst, chalcedony, citrine, daphnite, diamond, flint, garnet, holey stones, jet, lepidolite, nephaline, and ruby.

Dream Magick

If you have trouble remembering your dreams after you wake up, try sleeping with a piece of convoluted sheet quartz, jade, kyanite, or red jasper beneath your pillow.

To gain understanding of the messages and lessons conveyed during the dream state, sleep with a quartz crystal beneath your pillow. Be sure to position it so that it points toward your Crown Chakra.

Dream Spell (to Dream of a Certain Person)
By Judith Lewis

Items needed:

> 1 chunk of amethyst
>
> 3 rose petals
>
> 1 lock of hair from the person you wish to dream of
>
> 1 piece of daisy root
>
> 1 drop of rose or patchouli oil (optional)
>
> 1 pink candle

Perform this spell right before bed on a night of the new moon.

Take the amethyst, rose petals, lock of hair, daisy root, and empower all of them with what you want them to do (in this case being dream magick of a lover or friend). Place the amethyst next to your bed, atop it lay the rose petals, hair and the daisy root. If you wish, you may top it all off with rose or patchouli oil, and melted pink wax to fuse the items together.

As you lay yourself down to sleep, keep in mind the thought of the person whom you wish to dream about.

Fairy Potion Spell

To make a potion that will enable you to see the fairy folk, begin by pouring one cup of rainwater into a small bottle. Add three quartz crystals, three amethyst chips, one teaspoon of lavender flowers, and a few pink rose petals. Seal the bottle tightly and store it in a cool and dark place for three days and nights.

When you are ready to use the fairy potion, go into the woods, the garden, a field of wildflowers, or some other place where fairies dwell. Find a comfortable spot at which to sit, and allow your body to relax and your mind to be free of any negative thoughts or fear. Using an eyedropper, apply nine drops of the fairy potion to each of your eyelids. Take care not to get the potion in your eyes. After doing this, recite the following incantation:

With open heart and mind, I pray
My mortal eyes to see the fay.

According to fairy lore, the best times to observe fairies are at dawn, at dusk, and on the sabbats of Beltane (the first day of May), Midsummer, and Samhain (starting at sunset on October 31 and ending at sunset on November 1). However, it is said that the fairies most active during the "dark half" of the year (from Samhain to Beltane) are rather ill-natured and potentially dangerous.

Fairy Dust

To make fairy dust, put into a bottle 1 ounce each of powdered azurite, powdered quartz crystal, powdered malachite, powdered mica, and dried and finely ground root of mandrake. Add a pinch each of powdered frankincense, oak sawdust, ash sawdust, and hawthorn sawdust. Cover the bottle and shake it for a minute or two until all of the ingredients are well combined.

Sprinkle the fairy dust in your yard or garden, a forest, or any other area to which you wish to attract fairies. And as you do this, say aloud:

Wee folk of the fairy race,
I invite thee to this place.

Self-confidence

To magickally boost your self-confidence, wear a carnelian ring or pendant, or carry a carnelian stone in one of your pockets or in a small charm bag. Carnelian is also a good stone to use when one is faced with a difficult situation and feeling less than courageous.

Wearing a citrine on a necklace with the point of the stone facing downward is also said to benefit those in need of self-confidence.

The Crystal Pyramid Money Spell

To increase your money, perform the following spell on the first night of the waxing moon. Between two green candles, place a pyramid-shaped quartz crystal. Under it, place a brand new one-dollar bill. Light the wicks of the candles with a match, and, as they burn, visualize your single dollar multiplying into many. As you do this, recite the following incantation:

Pyramid and candle fire,
Money is what I desire!
Money, money, come to me,
As I will it, it shall be!

Continue to visualize your intent and chant for 15 minutes, then extinguish the candles. Repeat the spell each night until the moon has reached her fullest phase.

If your spell is successful, money (or an opportunity to make or earn it) will come to you before the next full moon.

Money Mojo Spell

To draw money into your life, wear or carry a green mojo bag containing a piece of turquoise and a silver Mercury dime wrapped in a two-dollar bill. Anoint the bag once a week with a bit of "money drawing oil" or any other occult oil designed to attract money.

To Secure the Love of Another

Perform the following spell on a Friday when the moon is waxing. Take two small heart-shaped pieces of pink wax and, using a pin or a nail, scratch your name upon one and the name of your love interest upon the other. Light two pink candles and hold the wax hearts over the flames for a few seconds until the wax begins to melt. Immediately join the two pieces together and, while concentrating upon the man or woman at whom your spell is directed, repeat thrice the following magickal incantation:

> *As these two hearts become as one,*
> *So shall the flame of love unite*
> *[name]'s heart with mine.*
> *Harming none, this spell be done.*

Wrap the wax, along with a piece of rose quartz and some pink rose petals, in a piece of pink satin. Secure it with a pink ribbon, and keep it in a secret place where it will be undisturbed. You will know the spell has taken effect when the lips of your loved one meet yours in a passionate kiss.

A Witch's Love Spell

To bring love into your life, perform the following spell on a Friday when the moon is waxing:

Using a silver pin, gently prick the third finger (the "ring finger") of your left hand. Take three drops of your blood and add it to 1 dram (1/8 of an ounce) of rose oil and mix well. Anoint a new pink candle with the blood-oil mixture, and as you light its wick with a match, repeat the following incantation:

> *By wax and wick and fire bright,*
> *The flame of love I light tonight.*

Next, place a heart-shaped piece of rose quartz at the center of a 9-inch by 9-inch piece of pink-colored fabric (such as satin, velvet, or flannel) and anoint it with the blood-oil while focusing on your intent. Place a lodestone atop the crystal and sprinkle some crushed rose petals or lavender over it while reciting the following incantation:

> *This amatory spell I brew*
> *To draw to me a love so true.*
> *From North and South,*
> *From East and West,*
> *Bring forth the one whose love's the best!*

After the candle has burned itself out, wrap the leftover wax, along with the stones, in the pink fabric and secure it with a pink string or ribbon. Hide it somewhere where it will not be disturbed, or bury it in the earth.

Note: Blood—the life force—is an extremely powerful magickal substance and has been used for centuries by Witches and sorcerers to empower all types of spells. However, some modern-day Pagans—particularly Wiccans—are vehemently opposed to using blood in their rituals. If you feel uncomfortable working with your own blood, you may opt to leave it out of the spell and use the rose oil by itself. Be warned, though, that the magickal potency of this spell will be greatly reduced if you do so.

An Ancient Spell to Bring Conjugal Love

As you visualize your intent, engrave upon a piece of beryl the image of a crow. Beneath it, engrave the image of a crab. Anoint the stone with three drops of rose oil, attach it to a chain of silver, and then wear it around your neck as an amulet to bring a love suitable for marriage.

A Dragon Love Spell
By Judith Lewis

To perform this spell, you will need the following: garnet, amber, citrine, malachite, lapis lazuli, rose quartz, amethyst, small clear quartz ball (best if it has flaws), nine apple seeds from an apple eaten at the full moon and dried for a lunar month, and nine rose petals placed under the apple seeds while they are drying.

Arrange the seven gemstones to form a circle, starting with the garnet in the north and continuing in a clockwise fashion. Once done, calm and center yourself by trying to clear your mind of all thoughts but your intention. If it helps, write your intent upon a piece of paper and just stare at it until your mind clears. Once you have focused on your intent, scatter the nine rose petals and nine apple seeds into the center of your circle. Spread the petals and seeds, place the clear quartz ball in the center, and then relax and concentrate. Nine times, repeat the following:

> *Petals from apples when the moon was on high,*
> *Sown with the bones of the dragons from Skye,*
> *Bring now unto me the love I desire,*
> *I'll cherish this love with a heart that's on fire.*
> *No one, this I choose, but to you send my plea,*
> *For I know not who the universe intended for me.*
> *Dragons in flight filled with magic to me,*
> *Bring forth my love now; help my sorrowful plea.*

To Ensure a Happy Marriage

On a Friday during a planetary hour ruled by Venus, take a piece of sardonyx (a striped stone formed from parallel layers of sard and onyx) and cut it into two pieces of equal size. If you carry one of the sardonyx halves with you at all times, and your husband or wife carries the other, it is said that you shall both be blessed with a marital union filled with happiness.

Sexual Magnetism Spell

An old Assyrian spell to cause sexual magnetism between a man and a woman calls for a piece of magnetite to be powdered and mixed with warm oil. Prior to sexual intercourse, the man rubs some of the magnetite oil upon his private parts, and the woman rubs powdered iron upon hers.

Warning: The application of such substances to the genitals can cause skin irritation and is, therefore, *not* recommended. Please note that this is a spell hailing from centuries past and is included in this book for historical purposes only.

Stone Spells for Female Matters

To ensure fertility, a woman should drink water in which a green agate ring has been washed. Also, the wearing of geodes increases female fertility and promotes conception, as does the carrying of naturally formed round stones and the drinking of potions containing powdered pearls.

To guard against miscarriage, many Witches in Macedonia have long prescribed the wearing of a lapis lazuli stone as a protective amulet. In medieval times, magician Albertus Magnus recommended the wearing or carrying of geodes as a preventative against an "untimely birth." To prevent a child from being born premature, a pregnant woman should wear an amulet made of onyx or sardonyx.

To ease the pains of childbirth and conduce delivery, a woman in labor should place a piece of magnetite, onyx, pumice stone, or sard on or near her. Some Europeans once believed that a small piece of malachite tied over a pregnant woman's umbilicus possessed the magickal power to facilitate childbirth.

To increase the flow of breast milk, an old Witch's remedy calls for a pinch of powdered milkstone (galaktite) or rock crystal to be mixed with honey and then taken during the waxing of the moon. A milkstone dipped in ocean water and then rubbed upon the breasts is also believed to produce an abundance of milk. Other stones reputed to stimulate, increase, and regulate the flow of milk in nursing mothers when worn or rubbed upon the breasts include the red jasper and serpentine.

A Spell to Recall Past Incarnations

On a night when the moon is full, light the wick of a purple candle and hold an opal to your Third Eye chakra. Sit comfortably, gaze into the flame of the candle, and allow your body to relax. Clear your mind of all distracting thoughts, and repeat the following chant (either out loud or to yourself) until contact with the psychic part of your mind has been achieved and past life visions begin to appear:

> *Earth and Water,*
> *Air and Fire,*
> *Let me know my lifetimes prior.*

Opal has been used by the Native American Indian and the Australian aboriginal Shamen to invoke visions; it has also been used during the Native American ceremony of the vision quest, and by the Australian aborigines during ceremonial dream time.

—Melody, *Love is in the Earth*

To See Ghosts

It is said that if you venture forth in the moonlight to a place inhabited by the spirits of the dead and gaze through a holey stone with one eye shut, their physical forms will be made visible to you. (Some occult practitioners believe that peering through a holey stone can enable one to also see mystical visions.)

Evocation of Spirits

Wear a jasper amulet (or any type of jewelry containing this stone) when performing any rituals involving the evocation of spirits. Many practitioners of ceremonial magick believe that jasper offers a magician protection against harmful spirits.

Spirit Oil

To make a powerful magickal oil to anoint gemstones and/ or candles for use in séances, necromantic divinations, and other rites involving spirit communication, you will need the following ingredients:

3 drops of mint oil

3 drops of sandalwood oil

1/4 cup of sunflower oil

1 Tbs. dried and powdered orris root (or serpentaria root)

1 Tbs. dried and powdered Solomon's seal

1 tsp. dried and powdered rosemary

pinch of powdered turquoise or jade (Note: Gemstones can be powdered by using a metal file.)

Combine the mint and sandalwood oils with the sunflower oil. Add the remaining powdered ingredients. Stir everything together for 15 minutes or longer as you visualize your intent of successful spirit communication, and then strain the oil mixture through clean cheesecloth into an airtight jar. Seal tightly and store in a cool and dark place for up to three weeks.

The Stone Circle Empowerment Ritual

To empower any object (such as ritual jewelry, a written charm, and so forth), gather together 13 stones: 12 holed stones and one heart-shaped stone.

Upon a consecrated altar, arrange the holed stones to form a circle and place the heart-shaped stone in the center. Light a cone or stick of frankincense and myrrh incense and pass thrice through its smoke the object you wish to empower. After doing this, place the object upon the heart-shaped stone in the center of the circle, visualize it radiating with a bright golden light, and repeat the following incantation:

By stone and circle and spoken spell,
May your power strengthen and swell.

A Magickal Oil for Divinatory Knowledge

To increase your knowledge and understanding when working with Tarot cards, crystal balls, dowsing pendulums, and other tools of divination, mix together the following:

1 dram of mugwort oil

3 drops of Mercury oil

a pinch of powdered blue obsidian

a pinch of dried and powdered eyebright herb

Prior to doing a reading or scrying, use a bit of the oil mixture to anoint a purple candle and your Third Eye chakra. If you so desire, you may use it to anoint your divinatory tools as well. Light the wick of the candle with a match and meditate for five minutes before proceeding with the divination.

For Good Luck

The luckiest stone in the world is said to be the black opal, and those who wear it are supposedly made immune to all bad luck. If you are unable to find a black opal, you can gain good luck by wearing an emerald on a Friday or carrying with you, in a charm bag, any stone that has been naturally formed into an L-shape by Mother Nature. For additional luck-drawing energy, be sure to add to the charm bag one or more lucky herbs, such as devil's bit, lucky hand root, or snakeroot.

The Lucky 13 Spell

When the 13th day of the month falls on a Friday, gather together one small piece each of the following 13 stones: alexandrite, amber, Apache tear, aventurine, chalcedony, chrysoprase, jet, lepidolite, olivine, opal, sardonyx, tiger's eye, and turquoise. Rub each of the stones upon the tail of a short-haired black cat, while chanting:

> *Image of Bast, goddess divine,*
> *Let good luck around me shine.*

Place the stones in a green mojo bag, along with a mint leaf and a pinch of powdered lodestone to act as a magnetic draw. Anoint the bag with three drops of "Lucky 13" oil (available at most occult shops).

Carry the lucky mojo bag with you at all times to attract good luck into your life, and to keep bad luck at bay.

Spell to Raise a Storm

Controlling the forces of nature is a traditional aspect of sorcery. Historically, storm-raising has been used for such purposes as to halt advancing armies and turn away pirate ships. Storm-raising has long been considered a sorcerer's ultimate display of magickal power.

To raise a storm using gemstone magick, place a large quartz crystal pyramid between your hands with its apex pointing down. Raise it to the sky and chant the following incantation while visualizing a storm unleashing its fury:

> *Pyramid of mystical form,*
> *Conjure from the sky a storm.*
> *Thunder rumble, cold wind wail,*
> *Fall to Earth the rain and hail!*

Continue chanting and visualizing your intent until the goal of your spell has been achieved. You will know that your magick has taken effect when you feel the breezes beginning to stir and observe the storm clouds gathering. (Note: The amount of time it will take to raise a storm varies from one spellcaster to the next, and depends on how powerful one's spellcasting abilities are.)

To Conjure Mist, Rain, or Snow

A simple weatherworking spell based on a centuries-old Chinese tradition calls for a piece of jade to be hurled with great might into a moving body of water.

Home Protection

To protect your home (whether it be a house or an apartment) against lightning strikes and destructive storms, keep a piece of carnelian (preferably one engraved with the image of a man holding a sword) on one of your windowsills as an amulet of magickal protection. Anoint the stone once a week with a drop of protection oil and thrice repeat the following incantation over it while visualizing your intent:

> *Stone of Fire, ruled by Sun,*
> *Let no harm by storm be done.*
> *Ward this home from Nature's furies,*
> *Keep those in it free from worries.*
> *As it is willed, so mote it be!*

Chapter 4

Amulets

"It is common knowledge of Magicians, that stones inherit great virtues, which they receive through the spheres and activity of the celestial influences, by the medium of the soul or spirit of the world."

—Francis Barrett, *The Magus or Celestial Intelligencer*

Planetary Amulets for Ritual Magicians

Amulets are beneficial for all ritual magicians—whether they choose to walk the left-hand or right-hand path—and the four essential ones that no practitioner should be without are a solar amulet, a lunar amulet, a Mercurial amulet, and a Venusian amulet. Ritual magician and author Steve Savedow says, "these four should be considered the minimum 'armory' of amulets any magician should possess."

The solar amulet, to be worn on a gold chain suspended from the neck, should consist of a solitary yellow topaz mounted in gold. It is vital that this amulet be acquired and consecrated on a Sunday, which is ruled by the sun.

The lunar amulet, to be worn (lower than the solar amulet) on a silver chain suspended from the neck, should consist of a solitary quartz crystal mounted in silver. It is vital that this amulet be acquired and consecrated on a Monday, which is ruled by the moon.

The Mercurial amulet, to be worn on the index finger of the left hand, should consist of a silver ring holding a solitary fire opal. It is vital that this amulet be acquired and consecrated on a Wednesday, which is ruled by Mercury.

The Venusian amulet, to be worn on the index finger of the right hand, should consist of a silver ring holding a solitary emerald. It is vital that this amulet be acquired and consecrated on a Friday, which is ruled by Venus.

According to Savedow, it is necessary to purify and consecrate these amulets on a regular basis, and, when not in use, you should keep them wrapped in white silk and hidden away someplace where they won't be disturbed. Wear the amulets only "when their effects are desired," and take care not to let anyone (especially other magicians) touch them or focus upon them, lest they be influenced "in undesirable ways."

You may wear either of the solar and lunar amuletic pendants solitarily or both of them simultaneously. However, the Mercurial and Venusian amuletic rings must always be worn at the same time, regardless whether you wear either, both, or neither of the amuletic pendants.

For more information on amulets, talismans, and ritual magick, I recommend that you read The Magician's Workbook: A Modern Grimoire *by Steve Savedow. (Publisher: Samuel Weiser, Inc.)*

Love-drawing Amulet

When worn or carried in a pink charm bag, a heart-shaped piece of carnelian, garnet, ruby, or any other semiprecious stone of red color works as a powerful love-drawing amulet for those wishing to attract a lover.

To keep its powers from waning, anoint the stone with three drops of rose oil every Friday at sunrise while you visualize your intent and three times say:

> *I call upon Venus, goddess of this hour,*
> *To charge this stone with love-drawing power!*
> *A magickal magnet it shall be,*
> *Attracting love's emotion to me.*

Amuletic Gemstones

Following is an alphabetical list of gemstones and their corresponding properties when used as amulets.

Agate

Agate is a semiprecious crystalline gemstone that is said to bring good luck, aid meditations, and guard against accidental falls and all types of danger. It symbolizes health and longevity and is a good luck charm for all individuals born in the month of June. Many Wiccans use agates in rituals to invoke the powers of the Goddess and the Horned God. In medieval times the agate was believed to bring down fevers, relieve thirst (when placed in the mouth), and protect against snakebites and stinging scorpions. According to an old Arabian legend, wearing an agate in the shape of an arrow purifies the blood.

Amber

According to Scott Cunningham, a prolific Wiccan author, amber "has figured in countless millions of spells and magical rituals." In ancient times, it was not uncommon for some men to wear amber amulets in the shapes of dragons, dogs, and lions to ensure sexual potency. For female fertility, women would often wear amber amulets in the shapes of rabbits, fish, and frogs.

In the Middle Ages, necklaces strung with amber beads were frequently hung around the necks of small children as amulets to protect them from, or cure them of, the croup (an acute inflammation of the windpipe, accompanied by a hoarse cough). Many New Age healers claim that amber strengthens the aura, and harmonizes and balances the yin/yang energies. Occult lore holds that it draws love (when worn near the heart) and sexual encounters (when worn near the genitals). It is also believed to attract compassion, ward off evil influences, and guard against accidents. As a healing stone, amber is reputed to bring down fevers, stop nosebleeds, and relieve such ailments as rheumatism, asthma, headache, toothache, earache, sore throat, and digestive troubles. In centuries past, the wearing of amber was even accredited with the power to cure insanity.

> *"A large piece of amber placed on the altar increases the effectiveness of your magic."*
>
> —Scott Cunningham

Amethyst

Amethyst symbolizes power, peace, protection, and spirituality, and many claim that it helps balance the aura, controls evil thoughts, reduces tension, sharpens the intellect, and brings contentment. In ancient times, amethyst was believed to possess the magickal virtue of preventing intoxication. Hold this stone in your hand or place it over the Third Eye chakra to aid spiritual and psychic development. It also acts as a powerful meditation stone. Wear or carry an amethyst amulet for prosperity, to ward off nightmares, protect against thieves, induce prophetic dreams, increase psychic awareness, enhance mental powers, banish sorrow, or overcome addictions. It is said that wearing an amethyst to court will influence the judge to rule in your favor. To shield yourself against psychic attack and negative vibrations, wear an amethyst pendant set in silver on a silver chain. An amethyst ring worn on the third finger of the left hand aids hunters and is said to keep sailors and soldiers safeguarded against harm. When engraved with the image of a Cupid, an amethyst ring is said to attract true love to the wearer. Amethyst is a good luck charm for all persons born in the month of February or under the astrological sign of Pisces. As a healing stone, the amethyst is reputed to relieve headaches and arthritis, strengthen the skeletal system, and prevent insomnia. Many New Age healers also use this stone to stabilize mental conditions and disorders of the nervous system.

Aquamarine

Aquamarine is a bluish green variety of beryl that is said to symbolize hope and good health. It is also used to protect sailors and other travelers of the sea. Wear an aquamarine amulet to enhance meditation and spiritual awareness, inspire courage, and prevent injuries (especially during military combat). To draw love into your life, wear a ring or pendant containing aquamarine. This stone is said to be a good luck charm for all individuals born in the month of March or October. As a healing stone, the aquamarine is reputed to be beneficial in treating swollen glands, improving poor vision, and maintaining healthy teeth and bones.

Beryl

Golden or yellow beryl is said to increase one's psychic abilities when placed over the Third Eye chakra or when held in the left hand during meditative rituals. Wear a beryl amulet to banish fear, strengthen the intellect, protect against enemies, and draw love. For centuries beryl has been used by seers as a speculum for scrying. Engrave the image of a frog on a piece of beryl and carry it near your heart or wear it suspended from a gold chain around your neck to promote friendship or to reconcile enemies. A beryl amulet engraved with the image of the Greek oceanic god Poseidon works as a powerful amulet of protection for those who sail the sea. As a healing stone, the beryl is reputed to be beneficial in treating concussions and disorders of the spine and heart.

Bloodstone

Also known as heliotrope, the bloodstone has been used by practitioners of the magickal arts for more than 3,000 years. It is said that the main virtue of this stone is to stop the flow of blood when applied to a wound, and it was for this very reason that many warriors in ancient Rome and Greece carried with them an amulet of bloodstone. Wearing a bloodstone amulet is believed to stimulate prophetic powers, avert lightning, conjure storms or earthquakes, and preserve good health. This gem has also been used to bring riches and good fortune, increase the fertility of crops, and secure victory in court and legal matters. For power over demons, medieval sorcerers are said to have worn a bloodstone or heliotrope amulet engraved with the image of a bat. Bloodstone is a good luck charm for all individuals born the month of March. As a healing stone, the bloodstone is reputed to bring down fevers, cure inflammatory illness, heal tumors, and prevent miscarriages.

> *"The virtue of the Heliotrope (Bloodstone) is to procure safety, and long life to the possessor of it."*
>
> —Leonardus

Cat's Eye

In ancient times, the Assyrians believed that the cat's eye possessed the supernatural power to make its wearer invisible. This stone is said to bring riches, attract good fortune, dispel negativity, stimulate intuition, protect against financial ruin, and ward off all forms of sorcery. It is an ideal stone to work with in rituals involving cat magick or felidomancy, and is popular among many gamblers (especially those who practice Hoodoo) as an amulet to bring luck in games of chance. Wear a cat's eye set in silver to keep from falling victim to the evil eye. As a healing stone, the cat's eye is reputed to cure all eye ailments, improve night vision, and relieve headaches, sciatic pain, asthma, and croup.

Chalcedony

Sorcerers have long revered chalcedony as a stone having great protective qualities. It protects travelers (especially seafarers), guards against accidents, and shields from psychic attack and all harmful spells dispatched by enemies. According to Melody, scientist and author of the metaphysical *Love is in the Earth* series, "It was used as a sacred stone by the Native American Indians, promoting stability within the ceremonial activities of the tribes." Wear or carry a blue chalcedony gemstone as an amulet to secure public favor, dispel melancholy, keep evil spirits at bay, and bring good luck into your life. To increase the supply of breast milk, according to an old belief among many Italians, nursing mothers should wear a white chalcedony amulet on a golden necklace. To ward off nightmares, night terrors, and fear of the dark, wear a chalcedony to bed or sleep with the stone beneath your pillow. Chalcedony is sacred to the Roman moon goddess Diana and should be worn or kept on the altar when performing any rituals in her honor. As a healing stone, the chalcedony is reputed to increase mental stability and be beneficial in the treatment of such ailments as dementia and senility.

Coral

In ancient times, coral was thought to possess the power to counteract poison, regulate the menstrual flow, protect sea-farers, and guard corpses from being possessed by evil spirits. According to the Roman naturalist Pliny, "Branches of coral, hung at the neck of infants, are thought to act as a preservative against danger." In the 16th century, it was common for coral to be powdered and added to Venus-ruled incenses, which were burned during the rites of amatory magick. Wear or carry a piece of pink coral as an amulet to draw love into your life. Wear or carry a piece of red coral to protect yourself against demonic forces, curses, and the destructive power of the evil eye. In Scotland, bells made from coral are used by some country folk to drive off evil spirits. Hang a piece of coral (any color) in your home or office as an amulet to keep evil spirits and nega-tive influences at bay; on your bedpost to ward off nightmares, nights sweats, and visitations by succubus or incubus demons; in your automobile to help guard against accidents and thieves; or on fruit trees to ensure their fruitfulness.

Black coral absorbs and transforms negativity, and is said to be effective in dispelling the fear of darkness. White coral helps to awaken or strengthen clairaudient abilities, while coral of a blue color enhances one's psychic awareness. Horn coral, which is also known as dragon's tooth coral, expands an individual's "knowledge of ancient civilizations and of the animal kingdom," according to Melody. It is also an ideal amulet to work with when getting in touch with your animal totem through ritual or meditation. As a healing stone, coral is reputed to cure indi-gestion, strengthen the bones and the circulatory system, stimu-late tissue regeneration, and nourish the blood cells.

> *"To be powerful in magic, ancient people used coral which hadn't been worked by human hands; that is, it wasn't polished, ground, cut or carved."*
>
> —Scott Cunningham

Diamond

Known as "the king of the crystals," the diamond is a highly valued gemstone that symbolizes peace, fidelity, innocence, and serenity. Its magickal and amuletic uses have been many. However, ancient legend holds that the mystical powers of this gem are activated only when it is freely given. In the Middle Ages, the diamond was used as an amulet against demons (especially the incubus), cowardice, plague, pestilence, and sorcery. It was, at one time, even thought to counteract poisons. According to medieval legend, to ward off enemies, madness, and all wild and venomous beasts, hold a diamond in your left hand as you recite the paternoster (the Lord's Prayer).

Wear or carry a diamond as an amulet to conquer infertility, reconcile quarreling lovers, prevent nightmares, balance both positive and negative energies, and inspire confidence, divine wisdom, and consciousness. To attract good luck, wear a diamond that has been faceted into a six-sided cut. The diamond is a powerful good luck charm for all persons born under the astrological sign of Aries. As a healing stone, the diamond is reputed to balance the body's metabolism, improve vision, fortify the mind, and strengthen the body. According to E. A. Wallis Budge, "wine and water in which a diamond was dipped preserved the drinker of it from gout, jaundice, and apoplexy."

Emerald

The emerald is said to symbolize peace, love, and eternal life. In the past it was believed that emerald amulets could calm storms at sea and protect pregnant women against miscarriages. The popular (although curious) belief that an emerald placed under the tongue could enable a mortal man to prophesy is one that dates back to ancient times. Wear or carry it as an amulet to bring good luck, dispel negativity, or strengthen love, intelligence, eloquence, and popularity. The emerald is believed to facilitate psychic awareness when held over the Third Eye chakra, and, when set in a ring of silver or copper and worn on a finger, it reputedly shields the wearer against poisons, strengthens the memory, protects against demonic possession, and ensures success in affairs of business as well as love. As a healing stone, the emerald is reputed to soothe the eyes, prevent nocturnal emissions (also known as wet dreams), and treat disorders of the heart, lungs, muscular system, and spine.

Flint

Also known as fairy-shot, elf-shot, and elf-arrow, the flint was once used in Ireland as an amulet for protection against mischievous fairies and elves. Shamans throughout the world have employed this stone in rituals to exorcise earthbound spirits from haunted places, and, according to Melody, "It has been used as a talisman to bring intellectual, psychological, rational, and physical strength during confrontations, arguments, and disputes." Wear or carry a flint as an amulet for protection against evil forces, to ward off nightmares, and to overcome shyness. As a healing stone, flint is reputed to treat kidney stones, skin lesions, indigestion, and disorders of the lungs and liver.

Fluorite

Also known as fluorspar, fluorite is a stone possessing stabilizing energies and the ability to strengthen the effects of other stones. It is said to increase psychic awareness and cosmic understanding when placed over the Third Eye chakra during meditation. Wear or carry fluorite as an amulet to bring order to chaos, improve concentration, strengthen analytical abilities, or encourage and sustain good health. According to Melody, fluorite can enable a person "to see both reality and truth behind illusion." Blue fluorite sharpens one's communicative skills; green fluorite eliminates negative vibrations; and purple fluorite facilitates clairvoyant abilities.

Garnet

The garnet is said to be a balancer of the yin and yang energies. It increases psychic sensitivity and sexual energy, protects the wearer from all dangers when traveling, and, according to a 13th century belief, repels insects. It is also an ideal gemstone to use during meditative rituals, and can be worn in the form of amuletic jewelry to attract sexual love or a soul mate. Place a garnet beneath your pillow to prevent nightmares and guard against evil spirits of the night. To draw good luck and ensure success in all endeavors, wear a garnet engraved with the symbol of a lion. Such amulets are said to have been popular in the Middle Ages. To attract a lover, wear a heart-shaped garnet amulet in a red velvet charm bag over your heart. As a healing stone, the garnet is reputed to treat such ailments as skin conditions and, according to Melody, "disorders of the spine and spinal fluid, bone, cellular structure and composition, heart, lungs, and blood."

Hematite

The hematite is said to enhance mental capability, balance the yin and yang energies, dispel negativity, and strengthen one's power of self-control when worn or carried as an amulet. A large piece of this silvery-black stone can also be used as a speculum for scrying. As a healing stone, the hematite is reputed to be beneficial in treating such ailments as insomnia, leg cramps, nervous conditions, anemia and other disorders of the blood. It is thought to draw disease from the body, and has been used by many New Age healers to help speed up the mending of broken or fractured bones.

> *"To ancients, hematite was what we now know as bloodstone, so virtually all magical information relating to 'hematite' in old books refers to bloodstone."*
>
> —Scott Cunningham

Iona Stones

Iona stones, which have long held a place in the folklore of the British Isles, are small green-colored stones that are found on the shores of western Scotland. Said to have been blessed by Saint Columba (who founded his first monastery on the Island of Iona in 563 A.D.), they are thought by some to hold the power to grant a solitary wish to any woman or man who wears them. These stones are also employed as amulets to attract good luck, as well as to safeguard the wearer against drowning. The healing attributes, if any, of Iona stones are unknown.

Jacinth

Known by the ancients as hyacinth, the jacinth is a transparent red, brown, or orange variety of zircon. This stone aids astral projection and increases psychic powers. It is often worn on a ring or carried as an amulet for the attainment of riches, honor, prudence, and wisdom. It is also reputed to protect against poisonings, lightning, thieves, injuries, and wounds. Wear a jacinth ring to dispel negativity and evil supernatural forces. To help ease the pains of childbirth, place a jacinth over the navel during delivery. In Italy, jacinth is used as the birthstone for persons born in the month of January. As a healing stone, the jacinth was historically said to draw pain from the body, stimulate the heart (when ground to a powder and taken internally) and counteract poisons.

> *"The jacinth possesses virtues from the Sun against poisons, pestilences, and pestiferous vapours; likewise it renders the bearer pleasant, and acceptable; conduces also to gain money; being simply held in the mouth it wonderfully cheers the heart, and strengthens the mind."*
>
> —Francis Barrett, *Natural Magic,* 1801

Jade

Jade symbolizes tranquility and wisdom, and in China it was once believed to impart immortality. It is also said to reflect "nine of the highest attainments of humanity," which are benevolence, knowledge, righteousness, virtuous action, purity, endurance, ingenuousness, moral conduct, and music. According to 7th-century philosopher Khivan Ghung, "It is this which makes men esteem the Jade as most precious, and leads them to regard it as a diviner of judgments, and as a charm of happy omen." It was once common for Chinese men and women to wear jade amulets in the shapes of various animals (particularly bats, bears, and birds) in the belief that they imparted longevity to those who wore them.

Wear or carry a piece of jade to attract love, guard against accidents, increase the amount of your wealth, preserve good health, or hasten the body's natural healing process. To prevent bad dreams from disturbing your sleep, wear jade to bed or sleep with a piece of jade beneath your pillow. To attract love and good luck, wear a jade amulet in the shape of a butterfly. And to prevent others from imposing their will upon you, carry a square piece of jade with the number 8 carved into one of its corners and the number 1 carved into the other three. (According to ancient occult tradition, for such an amulet to work, a magician must first exhale three times upon it and then chant the sacred name of Thoth—the Egyptian god of magick and wisdom—500 times at sunrise and again at sunset.) A jade statue placed in the house near a window or in the garden will avert lightning. To ease the pains of childbirth place a small jade figure of the Chinese goddess Kuan Yin over the navel during delivery. As a healing stone, the jade is reputed to stimulate healthy hair, soothe the skin, dissolve kidney stones, and treat disorders associated with the heart, hips, bladder, and spleen.

Jadeite

Jadeite is a form of jade, occurring in various shades of green as well as other colors. According to Melody (author of *Love is in the Earth*), it "was exalted by the Mayan and Aztec cultures as a stone of magic, bringing to fruition, in times of need, the protective forces of the ethers." Imperial jade, as the emerald green variety of jadeite is known, is beneficial as an amulet to improve dysfunctional relationships. Black jadeite is known to many in the occult world as the "devil's stone" and is often used by practitioners of black magick as an emitter for evil thoughts and curses.

Jasper

The ancient Egyptians are said to have used the jasper as a healing amulet, while the medicine men of some Native American tribes employed it as a magickal stone to bring rain in times of drought. The jasper is an energizing gemstone that balances the yin and yang energies, provides protection, and strengthens the intellect when worn as an amulet with certain Cabalistic inscriptions. It has long been used to counteract the power of the evil eye, ease the pain of childbirth, and protect the wearer against wounds and hemorrhages. According to occult lore, farmers in the agricultural regions of Italy once used black jasper to avert lightning. Green jasper is said to repel ghosts, bring down fevers, protect against the bites of serpents, and bring a restful night's sleep. Mottled jasper is worn to prevent drowning, and red jasper is used to deflect curses and psychic attacks. According to Scott Cunningham, "it sends negativity back to the original sender." It is important to mention that many people, including some Neo-Pagans (particularly Wiccans), feel that this type of magick is unethical because it causes harm to another. This property can be avoided by using an amulet with an alternate type of protective stone.

Jet

Known as the "Exorcism Stone" for its alleged power to exorcise both human and nonhuman entities, jet is actually a fossilized wood that resembles black glass. It was commonly used in the manufacturing of "mourning jewelry" in the Victorian and Edwardian eras, which led many to people to associate it with death, wakes, and funerals. Magicians have prized it for centuries as a stone of great protection, and, during the Middle Ages, it was worn as a traveler's amulet to guard against accidents, illness, animal attacks, and violence. It stimulates the awakening of Kundalini and is used in all Saturnian enchantments, such as spells to attract money or communicate with spirits of the dead. Wear or carry jet as an amulet to strengthen psychic powers, absorb negative energies, ward off the evil eye and guard against demons. Jet is the bringer of good luck to all persons born under the astrological sign of Capricorn. As a healing stone, jet was once powdered and mixed with wine to relieve toothaches. It was also powdered and mixed with beeswax to treat tumors. When worn, it is reputed to cure epilepsy, migraine headaches, swollen glands, stomach cramps, and even the common cold. Some New Age healers also prescribe carrying it to help alleviate depression.

Lapis Lazuli

Lapis Lazuli was a stone of great popularity among the early Egyptians, who used it to make blue eye shadow, and the Sumerians, who frequently used it in the making of magickal cylinder seals carved with the images and symbols of their deities. The Romans believed that pulverized lapis lazuli had an aphrodisiac effect when taken internally. They also used it as an antidote for poison. Ancient legend holds that an angel presented King Solomon with a magickal lapis lazuli ring, which allowed him to control the legions of demons that he used to construct his great temple. According to William

Rowland, a 17th-century doctor of physics, the lapis lazuli "is worn about the neck for an amulet to drive away frights from children."

This enchanting blue stone is said to work as a powerful love-drawing gemstone and one that strengthens the bonds between lovers. It promotes spirituality, aids meditation, and facilitates the psychic powers when placed over the Third Eye chakra. It is a popular amulet for amatory enchantment as well as protection against negative influences, psychic attacks, physical danger, and malevolent supernatural forces. Wear a lapis lazuli while you sleep to help you gain a clearer under-standing of your dreams. Lapis lazuli dispels melancholy and is also a powerful good luck charm for all persons born under the astrological sign of Capricorn. As a healing stone, lapis lazuli was once used in the treatment of such ailments as epilepsy, dementia, and diseases of the spleen. It is reputed to reduce fevers, strengthen the vision, overcome depression, relieve the symptoms of vertigo, and help mend broken bones. Some New Age healers also use it to treat disorders of the blood.

Lodestone

"Every Witch should carry two lodestones: One to draw things towards you and one to dispel psychic attacks, break negative shields, and ward off negativity."

—Silver RavenWolf

Magnetites possessing an additional property of polarity, called lodestones, have played an important role in Hoodoo and other folk magick traditions for many centuries. The ancient Greeks knew them as Heraclean stones. In olden times, amulets made from lodestones were worn to guard against snakebites, and it was believed that a lodestone placed in the right ear could enable a mortal man or woman to hear the voices of the gods. In the West Indies, it is common for many practitioners of Voodoo and Obeah to carry with them a red charm bag containing two lodestones—one for the drawing of good luck, and the other for the repelling of bad luck, curses, and evil spirits. In many parts of the world, the lodestone is also a staple of love magick. It is frequently worn in the form of amuletic jewelry or carried in a mojo bag with corresponding herbs and other magickal items to attract a lover, a spouse, or a soul mate. It also works for platonic and same-sex relationships. According to Leonardus in the year 1502, one of the virtues of the lodestone was to reconcile "wives to their husbands, and husbands to their wives."

Wear or carry a lodestone as an amulet to ward off hostile spirits, facilitate astral travel, strengthen the memory, draw good luck (especially in games of chance), and attract money. The lodestone has had many positive virtues attributed to it over the centuries, but, like many amulets of great power, it had its darker uses as well. In his book, *The Occult and Curative Powers of Precious Stones*, first published in 1907, author William T. Fernie, M.D. writes, "Marbodus has told curiously about the Loadstone, that if its powder be strewn secretly upon live embers, this proceeding will compel all the inmates to quit the house; panic struck, and thus allowing robbers free access into it unmolested." (Of course, this example is only for historical significance, and it is definitely not meant to suggest using lodestone in such a way.)

> "*Lodestone's basic use in magic is attraction. Because the stone is a natural magnet, it is manipulated in ritual to draw objects or energies to its user. Thus, it can be used in any type of spell.*"
>
> —Scott Cunningham

Many sorcerers of old were of the belief that every lodestone contained a familiar spirit, which gave the amulet its magickal potency. In order to prevent the power of a lodestone from waning, or to revitalize it, it was deemed necessary to "feed" the lodestone water and iron filings once a week on a Friday. Despite its peculiarity, this procedure is actually quite a common one in gemstone sorcery, although it varies slightly from one magickal tradition to the next. To preserve a lodestone's virtues, Monsieur Pomet's *Compleat History of Drugs* (originally published in the year 1712) instructed, "to hang it up by its equator, with a cat's gut, so that it may have its free tendency to the South."

As a healing stone, the lodestone was once thought to "bind and stop blood" (Dr. John Schroder, 1669), alleviate cramps, and relieve the gout (when burnt and made into a plaster with wax). In Cornwall, England, it was once thought that carrying a lodestone could cure sciatica. It is reputed to draw pain and disease from the body and work as a cure for such ailments as male impotency, rheumatism, and headaches. The lodestone is also said to strengthen the heart and assist in the healing of wounds. However, folklore holds that "it will not cure sores in the head during rainy weather" (from E. A. Wallis Budge, *Amulets and Superstitions*).

> "*It is said that, in 'days of old,' the lodestone was used to test fidelity; if unfaithful or un-loyal, one's wife, husband, or partner would 'fall out of bed' when touched by the lodestone.*"

> —Melody

Magnetite

See *Lodestone.*

Malachite

The malachite is said to be the guardian stone of travelers and children. Wearing a malachite amulet upon which the symbol of a rayed sun has been engraved has long been thought to increase a magician's magickal powers. Malachite protects against demons and bewitchment, and it is said that those who wear this stone will understand the language of animals and be safeguarded against falls. Melody calls it a "stone of transformation" and lists "the enhancement of psychic abilities" as one of its virtues. She also says that it offers protection to "those involved in the field of aviation." Wear or carry malachite to draw love, dispel melancholy, protect against physical danger, banish negative vibrations, or to ward off nightmares. The energies of this stone are also said to be beneficial for easing the pain of childbirth. As a healing stone, the malachite is reputed to be effective in the treatment of arthritis, asthma, and tumors. It has also been used for the mending of broken bones and torn muscles, and some New Age healers claim that it has the power to build up the immune system.

Moonstone

Carrying a moonstone, or wearing any type of silver jewelry in which it is set, enhances the feminine aspects of one's nature, draws love, offers protection against negativity and evil influences, enhances one's psychic abilities, and helps prevent insomnia. The moonstone is an ideal stone to use when performing spells and rituals in which lunar deities are invoked. Known in days of old as the "traveler's stone," moonstone has long been regarded as a lucky and protective charm for those who travel. The moonstone is ruled by the Element of Water, so if you have plans to travel over or on any body of water, be sure to wear or carry a moonstone to help keep you safe from whatever perils may lie in wait. Scott Cunningham suggested that swimmers wear a moonstone ring "for protection in the water." According to an ancient book of sorcery, placing a moonstone amulet in your mouth during the full of the moon will empower you with the ability to foretell the future. Wearing a moonstone ring helps to attract a soul mate, inspire tender passions, or protect a love. Carry a moonstone in a mojo bag to attract good luck or prevent nervousness. The moonstone is a good luck charm for all individuals born under the sign of Cancer.

Onyx

According to a 13th-century magickal treatise known as *The Book of Wings*, an onyx upon which has been engraved the image of a camel's head or a pair of goats among myrtles imparts to a magician the power to conjure and control demons. In the Middle Ages it was commonly believed that the onyx could induce nightmares and melancholy and even render its wearer vulnerable to the assaults of evil-natured demons unless it was worn with sard (also known as "sardius" or "Oriental carnelian").

To instill bravery, many magicians of old would carry a piece of onyx stone upon which was engraved an image of Hercules or the Roman god Mars. It is said that the onyx is a stone that absorbs and transforms negativity without storing it. One of its magickal virtues is protection, and, when worn or carried, it guards against psychic attacks. It is also capable of returning curses and negative energies to the sender, if programmed with such intent, although many view this as unethical.

Wear an onyx amulet to ward off misfortune, protect against danger, stimulate the mind, increase spiritual wisdom, or subdue the passions. The onyx is appropriate for all Saturnian magickal workings and dark moon rituals, and is said to be the bringer of good luck to all persons born under the astrological sign of Capricorn. As a healing stone, the onyx is reputed to strengthen the vision, end emotional suffering, cure epilepsy, ease the pain of childbirth, and heal ulcers and all wounds not inflicted by iron.

Opal

Sorcerers in ancient times are said to have used enchanted opals wrapped in fresh bay leaves to magickally attain invisibility. Wear or carry an opal as an amulet to facilitate astral projection, awaken or strengthen clairvoyant powers, balance the psyche, improve the memory, recall past lives, and attract good fortune. According to occult lore, the opal can also bestow healing power upon its wearer. This gemstone is ruled by lunar influences, and is therefore sacred to all gods and goddesses associated with the moon. The opal is a good luck charm for all persons born under the astrological sign of Libra, while the black opal (prized by sorcerers and Witches as a power stone) is said to bring luck to all 12 signs of the zodiac. Wear or carry a fire opal as an amulet to attract money, a blue opal to activate the Third Eye chakra, a red opal to reduce stress, an Andean opal to facilitate divination, and a water opal to stimulate psychic visions. As a healing stone, the opal is reputed to purify the kidneys and the blood, reduce fevers, strengthen the vision, and treat Parkinson's disease.

Pearl

One of the magickal virtues of the pearl is its ability to draw love, which is the reason practitioners of amatory enchantment (especially in the Orient) have valued it as a powerful amulet since early times. It was once common for women in Italy to wear pearls in their hair to ensure success in romance. In ancient Rome, dissolved pearls were often used as the main ingredient in love philters (potions). Wear pearls in the form of amuletic jewelry or carry them in charm bags as amulets to increase fertility, guard against shark attacks, strengthen physical powers, instill courage, protect against fire, banish demons, or ward off evil influences. According to the Hindus, the wearing of yellow pearls draws money. Pearls are believed to be the bringers of good luck for all persons born under the astrological sign of Cancer. As a healing stone, the pearl is reputed to be beneficial for aiding digestion, relieving biliousness and bloating, and easing the pains of childbirth.

Peridot

According to ancient magickal texts, a peridot set in gold protects its wearer against bewitchment, night terrors, illusions, and the evil eye. The ancient Romans are said to have worn rings of peridot to calm the nerves, dispel melancholy, and aid sleep. Wear or carry this stone as an amulet to prevent feelings of anger and jealousy or to draw the love of others. As a healing stone, the peridot is reputed to heal insect bites, facilitate the birthing process, strengthen the eyes, heal stomach ulcers, and treat disorders of the liver, spleen, heart, lungs, and intestines.

Quartz Crystal

Also known as "star stone" and "witch's mirror," the quartz crystal is a stone possessing great healing and occult powers. Despite its popular association with the New Age movement in recent times, the quartz crystal has been utilized by various cultures throughout the world as a tool of magick for thousands of years. The Cherokee Indians prized it as a divining stone, while many of the aboriginal tribes in Australia used it in weatherworking ceremonies to encourage rain in times of drought. *The Book of Wings* tells us that a crystal engraved with the image of a griffin (a mythological lion-like beast with the head and wings of an eagle) "produces abundance of milk."

Wear or carry a quartz crystal as an amulet to facilitate clairvoyance and divinatory abilities, aid meditation, induce prophetic dreams, ward off illness, and protect against psychic attack and evil spells. To understand the hidden meanings carried by dreams, sleep with a quartz crystal beneath your pillow. The rose quartz is potent as a stone of amatory enchantment and is often worn in the form of amuletic jewelry to draw love. Wear or carry tourmalated quartz to stimulate astral projection; rutilated quartz to amplify magickal energies during spellwork; and smoky quartz for grounding. As a healing stone, the quartz crystal is reputed to ease headaches and toothaches, relieve pain, reduce fevers, heal burns, strengthen the immune system, stimulate the thyroid gland, and treat respiratory ailments, vertigo, and infections of the bladder and kidneys. In some parts of Europe and the Middle East, it is also used to treat sterility and increase breast milk in nursing mothers.

> *"Ancient priests used quartz crystals to render negative energy impotent, to dissolve enchantments and spells, and to destroy all black magic."*
>
> —Melody, *Love is in the Earth*

Ruby

The ruby is said to be extremely lucky for all individuals born under the astrological sign of Leo. It brings peace of mind, stimulates sexuality, banishes evil and impure thoughts, guards against tempests, dispels sorrow, wards off unpleasant dreams, promotes good health, and increases one's physical strength. According to occult tradition, ruby amulets (especially rings) work most effectively when worn on the left side of the body. A heart-shaped ruby amulet attracts love when worn over the heart or carried in a red velvet charm bag filled with seashells and Venus-ruled herbs.

> *"A ruby set into a working tool of Fire, such as a wand, will amplify the elemental forces dramatically."*
>
> —John Michael Greer, *Natural Magic: Potions and Powers from the Magical Garden*

Sapphire

The sapphire symbolizes harmony and peace, and, when worn as an amulet, it brings happiness and contentment. This stone is said to possess the power to ward off bad luck, fraud, the wrath of enemies, violence, the evil eye, sorcery, psychic attacks, and accidental death. To acquire the power to see into the future, the *Book of Wings* instructs that a sapphire engraved with the image of an astrolabe (an instrument for finding the altitude of stars) be worn by the magician. This 13th-century magickal treatise also claims that when the image of a ram or a bearded man is engraved upon a sapphire, the amulet works to protect its wearer against demons, poison, and illness. Place a purple or indigo sapphire over your Third Eye chakra to facilitate psychic awareness or to gain insight to the future. Use a blue sapphire to promote dreaming or to facilitate the projection of your astral body. To dispel anxiety and calm the nerves, meditate while holding a blue sapphire in the palm of your receptive hand (the left hand if you are right-handed and vice versa). This stone is also believed to possess great healing powers and, for this reason, is often used in the laying-on-of-stones and as an amulet to banish, as well as to ward off, diseases. It is a good luck charm for all individuals born under the astrological sign of Taurus and all who are born in the month of April.

Wear or carry a black sapphire as an amulet to help you find or maintain employment; a green sapphire to help you remember your dreams; a yellow sapphire to guard against poverty and serpents; or a star sapphire to increase wisdom and attract good luck. As a healing stone, the sapphire is said to strengthen the heart, counteract poisons, heal boils and internal ulcers, reduce inflammations, treat disorders of the blood, and stop nosebleeds (when "laid to the forehead"). It was once thought to protect the eyes from small pox and other diseases. Yellow sapphire is used to treat ailments of the liver, stomach, spleen, and gall bladder, and, when taken as an elixir, is reputed to be effective in ridding the body of its toxins. Some New Age healers recommend the use of indigo sapphire for treating disorders of the brain.

Sardonyx

The ancient Romans were known to have engraved the image of the god Mars upon sardonyx amulets to provide courage. Sorcerers in 17th-century Persia believed that a thief could be made invisible to his victims by wearing a magick ring containing a sardonyx stone engraved with the image of a quail and a sea tench (a fish noted for its ability to survive outside water). When engraved with the image of an eagle's head, the sardonyx acts as a magickal magnet to attract good luck. Wear or carry a piece of sardonyx in a mojo bag as an amulet to attract friends, draw love, increase the mental powers, promote eloquence, heighten the senses, calm anger, gain self-control, and guard against the magickal workings of others. The sardonyx is said to be a good luck charm for all persons born under the astrological sign of Leo. As a healing stone, it was once used to remove rheum (a watery fluid secreted by the mucous glands) from the eyes, prevent premature childbirth, and dispel melancholy.

Staurolite

Cross-shaped staurolite crystals have long been employed as good luck charms, and it is said that the United States presidents Theodore Roosevelt, Warren Harding, and Woodrow Wilson each carried with them staurolite for good luck. In some parts of the world where witchcraft is feared, it is common for children to be given staurolite to wear about their necks or carry in their pockets to keep them safe from wicked spells and the power of the evil eye. According to Melody, staurolite "is used in ceremonies of 'white magic' and can facilitate the action of the rituals." Some magicians use it to ritually represent and exert control over the spirits of the four Elements. Wear or carry staurolite as an amulet to bring good luck, protect against accidents and evil, dispel negativity, and attract money. Some magickal practitioners believe that staurolite can also help one to break free from the chains of addiction. To attract benevolent fairy folk, wear, on a necklace, a green velvet mojo bag containing staurolite and white rowan tree blossoms. As a healing stone, the staurolite is reputed to relieve stress, dispel melancholy, reduce fevers, and treat malaria.

Sunstone

To invoke the mystical influences of the sun, many sorcerers in olden times were known to have worn an amuletic ring of gold in which a solitary sunstone was set. The ancient Greeks believed the sunstone possessed the power to counteract poison and bring physical strength to the body. It was used in India for protection against evil spirits, and by some North American native tribes in medicine wheel rituals. When carried or worn as an amulet, sunstone offers protection against negative energies, alleviates stress, and increases the libido (when worn near the genital region). The sunstone has also been used as a charm for gamblers, as it brings luck in games of chance. As a healing stone, the sunstone is reputed to be effective in relieving rheumatism, sore throat, and ulcers.

Topaz

Referred to as "one of the most well-omened of magical stones," by John Michael Greer in his book *Natural Magic*, the topaz has long been regarded as a stone of protection. When placed in the home, it guards against accidents and fires. When worn in the form of jewelry, it protects the wearer against black magick, injuries, jealousy, and madness. A topaz bracelet worn on the left wrist is said to keep away evil spirits, while a topaz ring worn to bed or placed underneath the pillow wards off nightmares and guards against sleepwalking. The topaz also works to draw love, promote courage, stimulate the intellect, and dispel negativity. In Africa, it is often used in healing ceremonies as well as in Shamanistic rituals to connect with the spirit world.

According to *The Complete Illustrated Book of the Psychic Sciences*, this stone "also is used as a divining rod to locate water, buried treasures, and precious metals." Topaz is said to be a good luck charm for all persons born in the month of November. As a healing stone, the topaz is reputed to aid digestion, stop hemorrhages, and relieve rheumatic and arthritic pain. In centuries past, it was not uncommon to find powdered topaz sold on the shelves of apothecary shops as an antidote to madness. When taken in wine, powdered topaz was, at one time, said to cure asthma, insomnia, and other ailments. Golden topaz is thought by some to be effective in treating ailments of the liver and gall bladder. Multicolored topaz is said to cure pneumonia, reduce inflammations, and regulate the proper flow of insulin to the bloodstream, while sheet topaz is prized by some healers as a reliever of headaches.

> *"The ancients supposed that the powers of the Topaz increased and decreased with increase and decrease of the moon."*
>
> —William T. Fernie, M.D.

Tourmaline

According to Wiccan author Scott Cunningham, the tourmaline was unknown to the magicians of old and is not a stone widely used by modern day practitioners of the magickal arts. This does not mean, however, that the tourmaline is without its fair share of magickal and healing attributes. Native American medicine men, African witch doctors, and Australian Aboriginal Shamans are said to have employed the tourmaline as an amulet for healing, as well as for protection.

Black tourmaline (like many black stones) absorbs negative vibrations and shields its wearer against wicked spells. When worn in conjunction with mica, it causes such spells to be returned to their original senders. Again, because some people view this type of magick as unethical, wearing the tourmaline without the mica will protect the wearer without causing harm to another.

Blue tourmaline, when worn over the Third Eye chakra, facilitates psychic awareness and induces mystical visions. Green tourmaline, which is also known as *verdelite*, increases the healing power of herbs, inspires creativity, and draws prosperity. Pink tourmaline calms, reduces fear, shields the aura against negativity, and induces peaceful sleep. Watermelon tourmaline heals the emotions, balances sexual energies, and stabilizes the yin/yang polarities. Yellow tourmaline stimulates the brain, strengthens the psychic powers, and increases both wisdom and understanding. Brown tourmaline, which is also known as *dravide*, is believed by some to possess the power to clear the aura and stimulate plant growth.

As a healing stone, blue tourmaline is reputed to be helpful in relieving stress and promoting restful sleep. For this reason, many New Age healers recommend it for persons suffering from stress-related illnesses and insomnia. Black tourmaline is used to treat arthritis and dyslexia. Green tourmaline is said to heal certain conditions affecting the eyes and be beneficial for shedding excess weight. Yellow tourmaline treats disorders of the gall bladder, kidneys, liver, spleen, and stomach. Watermelon tourmaline calms the nerves and aids the heart and lungs.

Turquoise

Known in Arabia as *fayruz* (or "lucky stone"), the turquoise is a mystical gemstone sacred to the Native Americans of the Southwest United States. It is highly prized as a luck-attracting stone and perhaps best known for its alleged powers to conjure rain and protect horseback riders from falls. The turquoise is said to possess the power to put wild animals into a hypnotic trance, ward off the evil eye, and protect against hostile magick, poison, the bites of reptiles, blindness, assassinations, and accidental deaths. Wear or carry turquoise as an amulet for strength and protection during astral travel, vision quests, and journeys through the unknown. This stone can also be used to draw love and increase psychic awareness. It is said to be the bringer of good luck to all persons born in the month of December. As a healing stone, the turquoise is reputed to relieve headaches, dispel melancholy, and cure cataracts. Melody claims that it gives strength to "the entire anatomy" and is good for all ailments, whether they be of a physical, mental, or emotional nature.

Zircon

The zircon is said to be the symbol of "innocence, purity, and constancy" (Melody). Sorcerers in the Middle Ages believed it to possess certain magickal virtues, including "procuring sleep, honor, and wisdom," (quoted from an unnamed magickal text in William T. Fernie's *The Occult and Curative Power of Precious Stones*) and it was once thought to counteract deadly poisons. The zircon has also been used in rituals to banish evil spirits. Wear or carry a clear (or white) zircon as a protective amulet against malicious magickal workings dispatched by enemies, a red or orange zircon to guard against injuries, a yellow zircon to stimulate the libido or to draw love, and a green zircon to serve as an amuletic money magnet. As a healing stone, the zircon is reputed to aid the mending of broken bones and torn muscles, relieve the symptoms of vertigo, and treat disorders of the sciatic nerve.

> *"The zircon is the stone of luck that grants the wearer all desires for health, prosperity, and honors. It is a silent protector against all dangers on land, sea, and air."*
>
> —Walter B. Gibson and Litzka R. Gibson

Chapter 5

The Curative Power of Gemstones

he public's interest in gemstones and their curative powers if often attributed to the so-called New Age Movement, which gained momentum in the 1980s. However, the idea of utilizing precious and semiprecious stones to heal the body, mind, and spirit is far from being a new one.

In *Harper's Encyclopedia of Mystical and Paranormal Experience,* author Rosemary Ellen Guiley writes that crystals were valued by ancient civilizations "for their alleged protective properties against diseases...and for their physical and mental healing properties."

It is believed that the early Egyptians, Babylonians, Africans, Mayans, Aztecs, Celts, Scots, Asians, Native Americans, Australian Aborigines, and other magickally influenced cultures of pre-Christian times ascribed medicinal values to certain stones.

Powdered pearls, which have been a staple of traditional Chinese medicine for thousands of years, have been prescribed to treat such ailments as epilepsy, heart palpitations, hyperactivity, and insomnia. Some traditional Chinese medical doctors also recommend them to quiet the nerves, heal inflammation of the uterus, benefit reproduction, and improve eyesight. Natural pearls are preferred over cultivated ones, and ingesting them is said to be completely safe and free of ill side effects.

Pearl powder also makes for an ideal beauty tonic, and is said to be one of the great beauty secrets known to women of the Orient since ancient times. When applied externally (usually blended with facial moisturizers), it aids the healing of blemishes, promotes the regeneration of cells, smoothes the skin, and diminishes wrinkles.

The quartz crystal was regarded by the Romans to be a natural pain reliever and an effective cure for glandular swellings and fevers. Surgeons in ancient Rome also utilized balls of crystal as lenses to burn out sores. Pliny, a Roman naturalist, wrote on this subject, "I find it asserted by Physicians that when any part of the body requires to be cauterized it cannot be better done than by means of a Crystal ball held up against the Sun's rays."

Scottish Highlanders believed the quartz crystal to be effective in treating kidney ailments. For this purpose they would set the stone in silver and wear it about the back.

In England, in days of old, it was common for many a village "wise woman" to treat ill children by rubbing a holed stone upon their bodies. A form of sympathetic magick, the action of this method was believed to transfer the disease from the afflicted child to the stone, thus allowing good health to return to the patient. After performing the healing ritual, the used stone would usually be cast into the sea or buried in the earth.

When the Black Death spread through Europe, China, and the Middle East in the 14th century (killing an estimated 40 million people), it was not uncommon for many individuals—especially those of nobility—to turn to gemstone amulets and elixirs in a desperate attempt to both prevent and to cure the plague. One of the stones believed to be effective for these purposes was the ruby.

In the book *History of Druggs*, originally published in 1669, authors Dr. Rowland and M. Pomet claim that garnets "cure palpitations of the heart; resist melancholy; stop spitting of blood; dissolve tartar in the body; and, when hung about the neck, are vulgarly believed to exercise these same virtues."

Gemstone healing takes many forms—from the wearing of amuletic jewelry (see Chapter 4), to the drinking of gemstone waters and elixirs (see Chapter 6), to the placing of certain stones upon the body's chakra points and energy meridians to alleviate stress and promote healing (the latter being known as the laying-on-of-stones).

The art of laying-on-of-stones is said to be rooted in antiquity. It is a popular healing method among many alternative healers in modern times, and can be carried out in several ways—either by using clear quartz crystals, colored gemstones, or a combination of the two. In addition, the stones can be used in conjunction with hands-on healing techniques (such as Reiki), chanting, prayer, and visualization, if both the healer and patient should desire it.

Some healers place the crystals and/or gemstones over the chakras that correspond to the internal organs or body parts in need of healing. Others place them directly over the afflicted area. It is a matter of individual choice, as there is no right or wrong way.

According to Melody, "There are no set procedures and no rules" when it comes to the laying-on-of-stones. Allow your own intuition to serve as your guide, and do not worry about making a mistake "because there are no mistakes." However, you should always use the appropriate stones in relation to the chakras of the hands and feet "to produce grounding to the physical plane."

In addition to facilitating healing of the body, mind, and spirit, the art of laying-on-of-stones can be employed to initiate astral travel, awaken psychic awareness, and so forth.

Many people believe that the healing or luck-drawing energies of many gemstones are most potent when they are worn on certain parts of the body. According to Kevin Sullivan, author of *The Crystal Handbook*, the forehead is the ideal place to wear fire agate, coral, and yellow jasper. The wrist is ideal for the wearing of amber, jet, and rhodochrosite. The fingers are ideal for the wearing of diamond, emerald (especially on the ring finger), lazulite, moonstone, opal (dark), blue quartz, ruby, sapphire, star sapphire, and topaz.

Stones for the earlobes include the apatite, bloodstone, fluorite, garnet, and picture jasper. Stones for the base of the spine are hematite and Herkimer diamond. Stones for the throat include the bloodstone, chrysolite, granite, picture jasper, jet, lapis lazuli, opal (dark or light), peridot, petrified wood, pyrite, and rhodonite. Stones to be worn over or near the heart include the chalcedony, garnet, picture jasper, lazulite, and ruby (which can also be worn on the ankle or a finger).

The following stones can be worn anywhere on the body: amethyst, citrine, jade, green jasper, magnetite, clear quartz, and turquoise.

Ailments and Their Healing Gemstones

The following list is included in order to give an example of the various ways gemstones have been used by magickal practitioners and alternative healers. It is not intended to be a guide to self-treatment, nor does it guarantee the effectiveness of any gemstone reputed to possess therapeutic qualities. In the event of a serious medical condition or emergency, it is recommended that you seek the help of a doctor, paramedic, or other qualified healthcare provider without delay.

Acrophobia (fear of heights): arthurite, heinichite, and linarite.

Addictions: amethyst (alcoholism), barite, dicinite (drug addiction), nissonite (alcoholism), smithsonite (alcoholism), smoky quartz, sugilite, thalenite (alcoholism), and zeolite (alcoholism).

Allergies: agate (dry-head), carnelian, clevelandite, cookeite, lazurite (food allergies), muscovite, palermoite.

Anemia: coral, hematite, goethite, leucite, magnesioferrite, meteorite, natrolite, siderite, and ussingite.

Arthritis: amethyst, chalcanthite, euclase, malachite, and tourmaline (black).

Asthma: amber, azurite, cat's eye, chrysocolla, clevelandite, malachite, morganite, tiger's eye, topaz, and vanadinite.

Biliousness: jasper, pearl, and ruby.

Bladder Disorders: amber, bloodstone, coral (red), cuprite, danburite, jade, jasper, manganite, obsidian (green), quartz crystal, sapphire (yellow), topaz (golden), tourmaline (yellow), and uvarovite.

Bleeding: chryoprase, feldspar (for nosebleed), hematite, lodestone, red jasper (for nosebleed), rock crystal, and sapphire.

Blood Poisoning: carnelian.

Boils: sapphire.

Bones: agate (blue lace), axinite, azurite, gyrolite, hematite, hodgkinsonite, lapis lazuli, magnetite, malachite, obsidian, pitchstone, quartz crystal (pocket), sandstone, seamanite, selenite, tiger's eye, and zircon.

Bronchitis: amethyst, chalcopyrite, pyrite, pyrolusite, rutilated quartz (needle stone), and rutile.

Burns: agate (flame), amethyst, carrollite, fergusonite, lamprophyllite, lavenite, quartz crystal, and rose quartz elestial.

Calcium Deficiencies: amazonite.

Canker Sores: fluorite and periclase.

Carpal Tunnel Syndrome: coral (horn).

Chicken Pox: agate (polka-dot) and childrenite.

Childbirth (to ease the pain of): agate, bloodstone, chryoprase, jade, moonstone, pearl, and peridot.

Circulatory Problems: coral and rhodochrosite.

Colic: coral (red), genthelvite, and nephrite.

Colitis: clevelandite, fluorite (green), kolbeckite, laueite, and opal (cherry).

Constipation: magnesioferrite and opal (cherry).

Consumption: see *Tuberculosis*.

Dementia and Senility: chalcedony and lapis lazuli.

Depression: agate (Botswana or regency rose), coral (red), garnet, idocrase (also known as vesuvianite), jasper (wonderstone), jet, lapis lazuli, manganosite, mordenite, opal (black), smoky quartz, and staurolite.

Diarrhea: ilvaite and rock crystal.

Digestion: amber, coral, flint, labradorite, obsidian, opal (black), pearl, and rhodochrosite.

Dizziness: lapis lazuli and rock crystal.

Ear Disorders: agate (angel wing), amber, atelestite, covellite, endlichite, goethite, kaolinite, obsidian, onyx, pachnolite, and quartz crystal (spade). See also *Hearing Disorders*.

Emphysema: agate (purple sage), chrysocolla, chrysotile (also known as chrysotite), fire opal, morganite, pumpellyite, quartz crystal (carbon-included), rhodonite, and williamsite.

Epilepsy: antlerite, jasper, jet, lapis lazuli, nadorite, onyx, pearl, quartz crystal (elestial quartz, also known as skeletal quartz), and selenite.

Eyesight: see *Vision.*

Fever: agate, amber, bloedite, bloodstone, bornite, carnelian, dicinite, hematite, lapis lazuli, magnesite, opal, pyrite, quartz crystal, rock crystal, ruby, sphene, staurolite, and zaratite.

Fingernails: agate (iris), moonstone, obsidian, sapphire, topaz, and tourmaline (watermelon).

Fractures: see *Bones.*

Gallstones: opal (golden).

Glands (swollen): amber and aquamarine.

Goiter: amber, thenardite, and zeolite.

Gout: amethyst, bornite, diamond, and joaquinite.

Headache: amber, amethyst, bixbyite, bustamite (for migraines), cat's eye, charoite, cornetite, dioptase, jasper (Arizona lizard stone), jet (for migraines), manganite, opal (cherry), parisite, quartz crystal, salesite, sugilite, topaz (sheet), and turquoise.

Hearing Disorders: agate, amethyst, Apache gold, bavenite, celestite, coral (horn), cylindrite, daphnite, graphite, harkerite, lapis lazuli, onyx, quartz crystal (spade or phantom), trona, and tsavorite. See also *Ear Disorders.*

Heart Disorders: agate, beryl, emerald, garnet, jacinth, lodestone, onyx, pearl, peridot, rhodonite, ruby, rhodochrosite, sapphire, and tourmaline (watermelon).

Hemorrhage: see *Bleeding.*

Hemorrhoids: bloodstone and heliotrope.

Hydrophobia (fear of water): ceruleite, hydrozincite, and natrolite.

Hyperactivity: pearl.

Infection: amber, amethyst, carnelian, emerald, jasper (bruneau), kammererite, marble, northupite, opal, penninite, sardonyx, smoky quartz, and stannite.

Infertility: coral, manganite, moonstone, sonolite, and tourmaline (orange).

Inflammations: angelite, boleite, brandtite, carnelian, bloodstone, emerald, erythrite, galena, garnet, lazurite, pyrite, rhodochrosite, sapphire, topaz, and williamsite.

Influenza (the flu): agate (moss), childrenite, fluorite, periclase, and pyrite.

Insomnia: amethyst, hematite, julienite, lapis lazuli, lodestone, mica (muscovite), moonstone, mottramite, parisite, pearl, sapphire, sodalite, topaz, and tourmaline (blue).

Intoxication: amethyst.

Kidney Disorders: bloodstone, chrysoberyl, flint, jade, opal, quartz crystal, rock crystal, and tourmaline (yellow).

Laryngitis: azurite.

Leg Cramp: hematite and magnetite.

Liver Disorders: agate (polka-dot), almandine, amethyst (chevron), aquamarine, azurite (combined with malachite), beryl, bloodstone, chrysoberyl, coral (blue), danburite, flint, fluorite (yellow), heliodor, iolite, jasper, lazulite, limonite, opal (red), quartz crystal (aperture), sapphire (yellow), strombolite, topaz (golden), magnetite, peridot, rhodochrosite, and tourmaline (yellow).

Lung Disorders: adamite, amethyst (chevron), ammonite, aventurine, chrysocolla, dioptase, emerald, flint, geode, kunzite, lazurite, mordenite, morganite, opal (Andean, pink, or red), peridot, pyrite, quartz crystal (aperture), rhodolite, rhonite, topaz (multicolored,) tourmaline (blue, pink, rubellite, or watermelon), and uvarovite.

Malaria: amber, Chinese writing rock, and staurolite.

Measles: agate (polka-dot).

Menopause: opal (cherry).

Menstrual Disorders: coral and malachite.

Miscarriage (to prevent): bloodstone and ruby.

Multiple Sclerosis: chrysolite and williamsite.

Muscle Spasms: amazonite.

Nervousness: amber, moonstone, sapphire, topaz, and tourmaline (watermelon).

Nervous System Disorders: agate (blue lace, Botswana, dendritic, or fire), alexandrite, amazonite, amethyst, azurite, barite, cat's eye, chalcedony, coral, cornetite, cumberlandite, galena, geode, gyrolite, hematite, lepidolite, nadorite, opal (dendritic or fire), and quartz crystal.

Neuralgia: carnelian and magnetite.

Oedema (Dropsy): amethyst.

Osteoporosis: amazonite, gehlenite, magnesioferrite, smithsonite, and strombolite.

Pain (general): rock crystal, ruby, and sardonyx.

Parkinson's Disease: opal.

Piles: see *Hemorrhoids*.

Poisoning: agate, diamond, emerald, malachite, sunstone, and zircon.

Poisonous Bites: amazonite.

Respiratory Tract Disorders: rhodochrosite.

Rheumatism: amber, carnelian, joaquinite, magnetite, malachite, melanite, sunstone (used by the ancients), and turquoise.

Smell (loss of sense of): jasper.

Sore Throat: amber, azurite, beryl, chalcedony, rhodonite, sunstone, tiger's eye, and turquoise.

Spine (to strengthen): magnetite and obsidian.

Stomach Disorders: agate, amethyst, beryl, heliotrope (bloodstone), jasper, labradorite, onyx, peridot, rhodochrosite, sunstone, and topaz.

Stress: apatite, aventurine, azurite, beryl, chrysocolla, diamond, fluorite, jasper, jet, lapis lazuli, malachite, onyx, pyrite, quartz crystal (blue), sapphire, and tourmaline (blue).

Sunstroke: brazilianite.

Taste (loss of sense of): topaz.

Tonsillitis: azurite, chalcedony, and pyrite.

Toothache: amber, aquamarine, malachite, and neptunite.

Tuberculosis: moonstone and morganite.

Tumors: bloodstone, jet, and malachite.

Ulcers: ilvaite, onyx, sapphire, and sunstone.

Vertigo: arthurite, cuprite, evansite, lapis lazuli, malachite, quartz crystal (clear, elestial, or spiral), rock crystal, rose quartz, and zircon.

Vision: agate, amethyst (for color blindness), aquamarine, aventurine, beryl, cat's eye (to improve night vision), diamond, emerald, lapis lazuli, malachite, onyx (for watery eyes), opal, peridot, tiger's eye, topaz (for failing eyesight), tourmaline (green), and turquoise (for cataracts).

Whooping Cough: coral.

Wounds: agate (plasma), bravoite, caledonite, carnelian, euclase, onyx (except for wounds inflicted by iron), quartz crystal, rutile, sandstone, topaz, and xanthoconite.

Chakras and Their Corresponding Gemstones

The following list contains the seven major chakras (invisible vortexes of energy located along the spine) and the gemstones that correspond to them.

☆　1st Chakra (also known as the Root Chakra, Base Chakra, or Kundalini Center): agate (botswana or fire), coral (red), flint, garnet (red), hematite, jet, obsidian (black), quartz (smoky), ruby, tourmaline (black), and all black and red stones.

☆ 2nd Chakra (also known as the Sacral Chakra): calcite (gold or orange), carnelian (orange or red), fluorite (red), garnet, heliotrope, jacinth, jasper (red), opal (fire), rhodolite, tiger's eye, topaz (golden), tourmaline (orange), and all red and orange stones.

☆ 3rd Chakra (also known as the Solar Plexus Chakra): adamite, amber, citrine, beryl (golden), jasper (yellow), laubmannite, malachite, peridot, serpentine, sunstone, tiger's eye, topaz (golden), tourmaline (yellow), and all yellow and yellow-green stones.

☆ 4th Chakra (also known as the Heart Chakra): alexandrite, amazonite, aventurine (green), bloodstone, chrysoprase, coral (pink), emerald, faustite, jade (green), kunzite, malachite, quartz (rose), rhodonite, tourmaline (pink and watermelon), and all pink and green stones.

☆ 5th Chakra (also known as the Throat Chakra): agate (blue lace or purple sage), aquamarine, azurite, calcite (blue), opal (blue), caledonite, chrysocolla, lapis lazuli, lazulite, lazurite, quartz crystal (clear), sapphire, sodalite, topaz (blue), turquoise, and all blue, blue-green, and blue-purple stones.

☆ 6th Chakra (also known as the Third Eye Chakra): amethyst, azurite, cat's eye, fluorite (blue, gold, purple, or white), labradorite (white), lapis lazuli, lepidolite, moonstone, quartz crystal (clear), selenite, sugilite (also known as luvulite), and all clear, white, and purple stones.

✩   7th Chakra (also known as the Crown Chakra):
    agate (angel wing), alabaster, amethyst, ametrine,
    diamond, fluorite (blue, colorless, gold, purple,
    or white), lapis lazuli, larsenite, quartz (laven-
    der), quartz crystal (clear), moldavite, moon-
    stone, and all clear, white, and purple stones.

Crystal Ritual for Self-healing

To perform the following ritual, you will need one or more
white candles, a stick or cone of incense, an athame, and a
piece of quartz crystal (preferably a self-healed quartz crystal,
which Melody calls "the master crystal in the art of self-healing").
If you desire, you may use any gemstone corresponding to
your healing need in place of the quartz crystal.

Begin by lighting the candles and incense. Using the
athame, cast a clockwise circle, beginning and ending at the
directional point of East. As you cast the circle, visualize it as a
glowing ring of white or golden light, and say:

> *By power of the silver blade,*
> *This clockwise circle now is made.*
> *Let it be a sacred space,*
> *Where healing magick will take place.*
> *As I will it, so mote it be.*

Empower the crystal by holding it in your power hand
(the right hand if you're a right-handed person; left if you're
left-handed) and visualizing it emanating with healing energy
in the form of a pulsating white or golden light. As you do
this, say:

> *By Water, Fire, Earth, and Air,*
> *By power of this Witch's prayer,*
> *By power of the gods that rule,*
> *I make this stone a healing tool.*
> *As I will it, so mote it be.*

Now sit in the center of the circle, either on a chair or a pillow on the floor, and face West (the direction traditionally associated with self-healing and wellness). It is important that you make yourself as relaxed and as comfortable as possible.

Take the crystal in your power hand and place it over your Third Eye chakra. Visualize a beam of healing light flowing from the chakra into the crystal, and then direct it from the crystal to the area of your body in need of healing. (For best results, it is recommended that you perform the healing light visualization for at least 20 minutes.)

To bring the ritual to a close, give thanks to the crystal for its healing power and then lay it down to rest. Uncast the circle in a counterclockwise motion with the athame, beginning and ending at the directional point of East. As you do this, say:

> *The circle once again is open,*
> *But its power stays unbroken.*
> *As I will it, so mote it be.*

Extinguish the candles with a snuffer or by pinching out their flames with the moistened tips of your thumb and index finger.

Repeat the healing ritual on a daily basis until your goal has been achieved.

Crystal Ritual to Heal Others

Prepare the ritual space, cast the clockwise circle, and empower the quartz crystal healing tool by following the steps outlined in the preceding "Crystal Ritual for Self-healing."

With the patient relaxed and sitting or lying comfortably at the center of the circle, take the crystal (or other empowered stone appropriate for the type of healing to be done) in your power hand and hold it approximately 12 inches above the affected area of his or her body, slowly moving it in a clockwise circle. As you do this, visualize healing energy in the form of a white or golden ray of light beaming from the crystal, and direct it into the area of the body in need of healing. Continue the visualization for at least 20 minutes, or until the time that you intuitively feel the patient's body has received the energy it needed.

To bring the ritual to a close, follow the steps also outlined above in the "Crystal Ritual for Self-healing." Repeat this ritual on a daily basis until the patient is completely recovered, or whenever it is felt that healing energy is needed.

Tips for Crystal and Gemstone Healing

☆ Unplug or turn off the ringer of the telephone before performing a healing ritual so you and your patient will not be disturbed by its ringing.

☆ Before lighting incense or smudge bundles, it is a good idea to check with your patient and find out if he or she has any health conditions (such as allergies, asthma, or sensitive eyes) that could be aggravated by the inhalation of smoke.

☆ Some types of background music can aid a healing ritual by creating a peaceful mood. Music that is soft and soothing brings relaxation to the body and mind, and also makes one more receptive to magickal healing energies.

☆ The sound of moving water (such as flowing fountains, ocean waves, and the gentle pitter-patter of falling raindrops) also induces a relaxed state in most people and facilitates the healing process.

☆ Healing energy is absorbed with full potency when the area of the body being treated is exposed, as opposed to being covered. Clothing and other coverings (such as blankets) creates a barrier between the patient and the healer's crystal, filtering out portions of the healing energy beam and thus reducing its effectiveness in relieving pain, healing wounds, and treating illness.

☆ When working with a terminated quartz crystal (one with a pointed end), be sure to hold it so that it termination points down toward the body. This directs the healing energy to the area where it is needed. However, to draw out from the body (fever or infections, for example), hold the crystal so that its termination points away from the body.

☆ To add extra healing power, an appropriate essential oil or gem essence can be applied directly to a quartz crystal or gemstone prior to the start of a healing ritual.

Chapter 6

Elixirs and Potions

Gemstone elixirs (also known as gemstone tinctures, gemstone essences, gemstone remedies, or lapidary waters) are preparations that are made in a manner similar to that of flower essences. They also work in much the same way. Like other holistic remedies, gemstone elixirs are said to treat the root of the problem instead of just the symptoms associated with it. Gemstone elixirs can be instrumental in clearing a blocked energy flow in an unhealthy individual, thereby allowing his or her healing process to work faster and more efficiently.

Elixirs that are made with gemstones are believed to contain the essence, or vibration, of the stone with which it was prepared. More than one gemstone essence can be used in the making of such an elixir; however, all stones that are used should always be cleaned and charged prior to being used.

To "charge" a gemstone basically means to program it with your energy. The method is very simple: Place the stone in the palm of your power hand (the right hand if you are a right-handed individual; the left hand if you are a left-handed one) and concentrate on the goal, visualizing energy in the form of white light flowing from your hand into the stone. The amount of time required to charge a stone depends upon the individual. It may take a few minutes or half an hour or longer. Most magickal practitioners are able to sense when a stone is vibrating with their personal power, and that is how they are able to determine when the charging process is complete.

To make a gemstone elixir, you will need water (spring is best, but distilled water can also be used), brandy (which can be substituted with vegetable glycerin or apple cider to act as a preservative), and one or more gemstones appropriate to your needs. For instance, a bloodstone for treating diseases of the blood, a beryl for treating disorders of the heart and spine, an Apache tear (a globule of translucent obsidian) for healing the emotions, and so forth.

Place the crystal or gemstone in a sterilized glass jar and fill it with spring water. Cover the jar and then place it outside to absorb the rays of the sun from sunrise until sunset. For best results, it is recommended that you do this on a day when the phase of the moon is full or new. Bring the jar of gemstone water indoors and remove the gemstone. (To make an elixir containing only lunar energies, which are beneficial for healing the emotions, place the jar outside at night to absorb the rays of the full moon. To capture both lunar and solar energies, leave the jar outside for one full day and night.)

Some magickal practitioners leave their gemstone water outside for seven days before bringing it indoors where it is stored away from light for another seven days before being used. And some also find that by having seven quartz points positioned around the stored jar with their pointed ends facing inward greatly increases the potency of the elixir.

The next step calls for a dark colored glass bottle to be placed in boiling water for 15 minutes in order to sterilize it. Bottles with plastic eyedroppers are not recommended. Remove the sterilized bottle from the water and then fill it with equal parts of gemstone water and brandy (or other preservative mentioned previously). Seal the bottle with a tight-fitting lid and keep it in a cabinet or on a shelf away from direct sunlight.

Shake the bottle for one to two minutes before each use to reactivate the energies within the elixir, and then place three to five drops under your tongue while concentrating upon the healing of your ailment and visualizing yourself in a state of wellness. You may also offer a personal prayer to the god or goddess of your belief system and/or recite an incantation if you feel in your heart that it will help to strengthen the healing power of the elixir. Repeat the dosage four times a day for as long as needed.

Some Witches and New Age alternative healers have found that using a dowsing pendulum or other method of divination is effective in determining the number of dosages that should be taken each day.

Please note: While gemstone elixirs can be beneficial for certain individuals, they are not intended to take the place of proper medical care. It is also important to note that gemstone elixirs made with alcohol should not be used by persons with an alcohol dependency problem or by anyone taking medication that calls for the avoidance of alcohol. (If in doubt, always check with your doctor or pharmacist first, because the effects of certain prescription and over-the-counter drugs are weakened by alcohol, and some are dangerously intensified. Other pharmaceuticals, when mixed with alcohol, can even cause coma or death.) For all serious medical conditions, whether they are of a physical, mental, or emotional nature, the author and publisher of this book strongly recommend that you seek medical attention from a qualified medical practitioner without delay.

Like flower essences, the number of ways in which gemstone elixirs can be used is practically unlimited. For instance, adding 20 drops to your bath water enables your body to absorb the gemstone energy directly through the skin. Gemstone elixirs can be added to your favorite massage oil and then massaged into the body's chakras or affected areas. They can also be put into an atomizer bottle and used to spray a room or mist one's aura with gemstone energy.

Add three drops of an appropriate gemstone elixir to occult oils for anointing spell candles, altar tools, and poppets. (For instance, use a rose quartz elixir for love spells, a turquoise elixir for protection spells, a moonstone elixir for divinatory rituals or spells concerning clairvoyance, and so forth.)

Before painting or wallpapering a room, stir 2 ounces (1/4 cup) of gemstone elixir into a gallon of water-based paint or wallpaper glue to fill the redecorated room with beneficial gemstone vibrations.

In addition, gemstone elixirs can be employed to heal pets and familiars. (For further information on this, see the following section.)

Gemstone Elixirs for Animals

The healing power of gemstone elixirs can be used to benefit animals (both pets and familiars) as well as humans. To make a gemstone elixir for an animal, follow the instructions outlined previously, but reduce the amount of alcohol to 2 percent.

For birds, add a few drops of gemstone elixir to drinking water or use a spray bottle to spray the elixir around the cage. Take care not to spray it directly into a bird's mouth. For animals such as cats and dogs, add a few drops of gemstone elixir to the animal's food or drinking water, or apply externally to the animal's chakras. (It is said that animals possess five major chakras along the spine, unlike humans, who possess seven. In animals, the Root Chakra is located at the base of the spine, the Solar Plexus Chakra at the upper part of the back, the Heart Chakra at the center of the rib cage, the Throat Chakra at the middle of the neck, and a chakra combining the equivalent of the human Crown and Third Eye at the top of the head. In addition, animals possess smaller energy points that are located in the paw pads, the ears, and the tip of the tail.)

The following examples show the different ways in which gemstone elixirs can be used for animals:

Amethyst Elixir: said to be useful for calming overly stressed or hyperactive animals, as well as for preventing flea infestations.

Bloodstone Elixir: said to work well in raising a sluggish animal's energy level. In addition, they are reputed to strengthen the heart and instill courage.

Citrine Elixir: believed to help speed up the body's healing process and are ideal for treating a sick or injured animal.

Lepidolite Elixir: often given to rescued cats and dogs (and other animals) to help them adjust to their new homes and build trust toward their new human guardians.

Moldavite Elixir: said to stimulate an animal's keen psychic ability and help to create a powerful psychic bond between animals and humans.

Moonstone Elixir: reputedly most beneficial for animals of the female gender, enhancing well-being in all aspects of female reproduction.

Quartz (Rose) Elixir: said to bring about a more loving nature in many cats and dogs possessing an unfriendly disposition. It will also help an abused and/or neglected animal overcome its feelings of insecurity and mistrust of humans.

Triple Gemstone Elixirs

Triple gemstone elixirs are tinctures containing three different gems. They are made and used in precisely the same fashion as regular gemstone elixirs, however, some people feel that they are three times more powerful than gemstone elixirs made with just a single stone.

To make a triple gemstone elixir for:

Calming Fear: use the following three stones: mica, sunstone, and tourmaline.

Drawing Love: use the following three stones: barite, blue topaz, and purple chevron amethyst.

Healing the Body, Mind, and Spirit: use the following three stones: garnet, green calcite, and selenite.

Increasing Psychic Awareness: use the following three stones: apophyllite, blue lace agate, and purple fluorite.

Mending a Broken Heart: use the following three stones: blue calcite, chrysocolla, and rose quartz.

Power-raising: use the following three stones: carnelian, mahogany obsidian, and meteorite.

Prosperity: use the following three stones: citrine, moss agate, and tiger's eye.

Protection Against Evil and Harm: use the following three stones: onyx, red jasper, and smoky quartz.

Stimulating Erotic Passion: use the following three stones: fire agate, onyx, and red jasper.

Warning: Not all stones are suitable for making elixirs. Substances in some stones can produce unsafe solutions (such as acids) when they react with water. Those containing any kind of metal (such as copper or lead) should not be used, as they can be toxic to both humans and animals. (Many of the blue and green stones—especially those that are brightly colored—contain varying amounts of copper.)

The Following Stones Should Be Avoided:

Amazonite (contains traces of copper)

Atacamite (contains copper)

Auricalcite (contains zinc and copper)

Azurite (contains copper)

Boji-stones (contains some sulfur)

Bronchantite (contains copper)

Chalcantite (contains copper)

Chalcopyrite (contains copper and sulfur)

Cinnabar (contains mercury)

Conicalcite (contains copper)

Crysocolla (contains copper)

Cuprite (contains copper)

Dioptase (contains copper)

Fool's Gold (see *Pyrite*)

Gem Silica (contains copper)

Galena/Galenite (contains almost 90 percent lead)

Garnierite (contains nickel)

Lapis Lazuli (pyrite inclusions contain sulfur)

Malachite (contains copper)

Markasite (contains sulfur)

Mohawkite (contains copper and arsenic)

Psiomelan (contains barium)

Pyrite (contains sulfur)

Realgar (contains sulfur and arsenic)

Stibnite (contains lead)

Smithsonite (contains zinc and copper)

Vanadanite (contains lead)

Wulfenite (contains lead and molybdenum)

Additionally, hematite and magnetite should not be used for gemstone elixirs due to their tendency to rust when placed in water.

Lunar Water Tonic

To create a simple, yet powerful, lunar water tonic to help rejuvenate your body, mind, and spirit, place one or more pieces of quartz crystal that have been thoroughly cleaned and cleared of all negative vibrations in a clear glass container. Fill the container with spring water, cover it with a magnifying glass, and then place it outside to absorb the rays of the full moon. (Note: The longer you leave it exposed to moonlight, the greater its lunar potency will be. Take care, however, to bring the water indoors before the first light of dawn appears at the eastern horizon.)

Remove the magnifying glass and quartz crystal (or crystals) from the glass container after bringing it in. Cover the container with a lid and keep it stored in the refrigerator to prevent the water from stagnating.

It is recommended that you drink a small amount of the tonic every morning upon waking and every evening before retiring. You may also use it any time you feel yourself to be in need of rejuvenation.

Lunar water tonic is also beneficial when taken prior to crystal gazing and other divinatory work, as the mystical energies of both the quartz crystal and the full moon have long been credited with the ability to stimulate psychism. It can also be poured into a black cauldron and used for scrying purposes.

Lunar water tonic has many other usages in addition to the ones just given, such as benefiting pets and plants. I often give lunar water tonic to my cats to help keep them healthy and frisky. And I know several "Green" Witches who regularly water their herb gardens and houseplants with it and claim that it stimulates plant growth and intensifies a plant's inherent magickal energies. In addition, it can be added to baths, used in cooking, and so forth.

Chapter 7

Stones of
the Zodiac

ach of the 12 astrological signs of the zodiac is said to rule one or more gemstone, known as a "birth-charm," "birth-stone," "natal stone," or "zodiacal gem." These gemstones are frequently carried in mojo bags or worn in the form of amuletic jewelry to draw good luck to the wearer, as well as to guard against evil forces, misfortune, and illness. However, many superstitious people consider it to be extremely unlucky to wear a birth charm belonging to an astrological sign other than their own.

"Birthstones have been worn as a lucky charm by both men and women through many centuries."

—Walter B. Gibson and Litzka R. Gibson, *The Complete Illustrated Book of the Psychic Sciences*

The Origin of Birthstones

Birthstones have a long and interesting history. They are believed to have been originally employed as amulets to ward off disease and as facilitators to bring about the wearer's wishes. As time marched on, various myths and legends, as well as symbolic meanings became attached to them. By the late 18th century, their use was no longer confined to clandestine occult circles, and many persons (men and women alike) took to wearing the gems of their zodiac signs for good luck. Since then, the widespread popularity of birthstones has never waned and is perhaps even more popular now than ever before.

Some individuals, particularly those of narrow mind, dismiss the occult properties of birthstones (and other gems as well) as nothing more than mere superstition carried over from olden times. However, many occult practitioners and others continue to hold steadfast onto the old belief that certain precious stones contain inherent mystical vibrations that correspond to the 12 months of the year and to the 12 astrological signs of the zodiac.

Biblical Birthstones

According to the Gemological Institute of America, the origin of the western system of birthstones can be traced back to biblical times—and specifically to the Breastplate of Aaron. (Aaron was a Hebrew High Priest and the brother of Moses.) Also known as the Breastplate of the High Priest, this legendary religious caftan is said to be one of the oldest amulets known to man. According to the Bible (in which various precious stones are mentioned more than 200 times), it was made with the following gems: sardius (also known as sard, another name for carnelian), topaz, carbuncle, emerald, sapphire, diamond, ligure, agate, amethyst, beryl, onyx, and jasper (from Exodus 28, 15:30).

In The Complete Book of Amulets and Talismans, author Migene Gonzalez-Wippler writes, "The 12 stones represented alternatively the 12 tribes of Israel, the 12 months of the year, and the 12 signs of the zodiac."

Another of the earliest references to stones can be found in the Book of Revelations. In Revelations 21:18-21, the 12 foundations of the city wall of the New Jerusalem that descends from heaven are said by Saint John to be made of various gemstones:

> *And the building of the wall of it was of jasper: and the city was pure gold, like unto clear glass. And the foundations of the wall of the city were garnished with all manner of precious stones. The first foundation was jasper; the second, sapphire; the third, a chalcedony; the fourth, an emerald; the fifth, sardonyx; the sixth, sardius; the seventh, chrysolyte; the eighth, beryl; the ninth, a topaz; the tenth, a chrysoprasus; the eleventh, a jacinth; the twelfth, an amethyst. And the twelve gates were twelve pearls: every several gate was of one pearl: and the street of the city was pure gold, as if it were transparent glass.*

The "12 magical gems" described in the Book of Revelations were catalogued by Jewish historian, Flavius Josephus (37 A.D.—circa 101 A.D.), who is believed to be the first author on this subject. In the fifth century, when Saint Jerome wrote of birthstones, he drew a comparison between these gems and the ones worn in the breastplate of the High Priest. (Note: The ancients were known to have classified their gemstones primarily by color instead of by their mineral and chemical properties. This has caused considerable disagreement among some historians and occultists as to the modern names for the precious stones that were set in the Breastplate of the High Priest. As a result, different authorities over the years have assigned different gems to the various months, astrological signs, and so forth. And to add to the bewilderment, many jewelers have devised their own lists of monthly and zodiacal birthstones.)

Around the 8th or 9th century, interpreters of the Book of Revelations began to ascribe to these 12 precious stones the attributes of the 12 apostles. The correspondences are as follows:

Apostle	Gemstone
St. Andrew	Sapphire
St. Bartholomew	Sardius (Carnelian)
St. James	White Chalcedony
St. James the Less	Topaz
St. John	Emerald
St. Matthew	Amethyst
St. Matthias	Chrysolite
St. Peter	Jasper
St. Phillip	Sardonyx
St. Simeon	Jacinth
St. Thaddeus	Chrysoprase
St. Thomas	Beryl

Mystical Birthstones

The two main categories under which birthstones fall are *Monthly* (which ascribes gems to the birth month) and *Zodiacal* (which ascribes gems to the astrological sign of the zodiac).

Monthly birthstones, as a rule, fit into one or more of the lists shown on the chart that follows. The first (*Modern*) is a list that was officially adopted by both the American National Association of Jewelers and the Jewelers of America on August 12, 1912. The second (*Traditional*) is an earlier version of the Modern birthstone list and is based on societal birthstone traditions dating from the 5th century to the present. The third (*Mystical*) is loosely based on a 1,000-year-old list that originated in Tibet. *Ayurvedic* birthstones are from a list of gems used in *Ayurveda*—a holistic system of medicine that originated in India thousands of years ago. Traditional Hebrew, Arabic, and Roman lists are included as well.

Monthly Birthstones

Month	Modern	Traditional	Mystical	Ayurvedic	Hebrew	Arabic	Roman
January	Garnet	Garnet	Emerald	Garnet	Garnet	Garnet	Jacinth or Garnet
February	Amethyst	Amethyst	Bloodstone	Amethyst	Amethyst	Amethyst	Amethyst
March	Bloodstone or Aquamarine	Bloodstone	Jade	Bloodstone	Bloodstone	Bloodstone	Bloodstone
April	Diamond	Diamond	Opal	Diamond	Sapphire	Sapphire	Sapphire
May	Emerald	Emerald	Sapphire	Agate	Agate	Emerald	Agate
June	Pearl or Moonstone	Alexandrite	Moonstone	Pearl	Emerald	Agate	Emerald
July	Ruby	Carnelian	Ruby	Ruby	Onyx	Carnelian	Onyx
August	Peridot or Sardonyx	Sardonyx	Diamond	Sapphire	Carnelian	Sardonyx	Carnelian
September	Sapphire	Sapphire	Agate	Moonstone	Peridot	Peridot	Chrysolite or Peridot
October	Opal or Pink Tourmaline	Tourmaline	Jasper	Opal	Aquamarine	Aquamarine	Aquamarine
November	Yellow Topaz or Citrine	Citrine	Pearl	Topaz	Topaz	Topaz	Topaz
December	Zircon or Turquoise	Turquoise	Onyx	Ruby	Ruby	Ruby	Ruby

Zodiacal Birthstones

The 12 astrological signs of the zodiac and their corresponding birthstones are as follows:

Zodiacal Sign	Dates	Birthstone(s)
Aries ♈	Mar 21–Apr 19	Coral and Diamond
Taurus ♉	Apr 20–May 20	Carnelian and Emerald
Gemini ♊	May 21–Jun 20	Agate and Alexandrite
Cancer ♋	Jun 21–Jul 22	Moonstone, Pearl, and all white-colored gemstones
Leo ♌	Jul 23–Aug 22	Amber, Ruby, and yellow or golden-colored gemstones
Virgo ♍	Aug 23–Sep 22	Sapphire and Sardonyx
Libra ♎	Sep 23–Oct 22	Opal and Tourmaline
Scorpio ♏	Oct 23–Nov 21	Topaz
Sagittarius ♐	Nov 22–Dec 21	Turquoise and Zircon
Capricorn ♑	Dec 22–Jan 20	Garnet, Lapis Lazuli, and all black gemstones
Aqarius ♒	Jan 21–Feb 18	Amethyst and Jacinth
Pisces ♓	Feb 19–Mar 20	Aquamarine and Bloodstone

Gemstones for the Hour of Birth

The following chart lists the corresponding gemstone for the hour within which you were born.

1 a.m.	Quartz		1 p.m.	Zircon
2 a.m.	Hematite		2 p.m.	Emerald
3 a.m.	Malachite		3 p.m.	Beryl
4 a.m.	Lapis Lazuli		4 p.m.	Topaz
5 a.m.	Turquoise		5 p.m.	Ruby
6 a.m.	Tourmaline		6 p.m.	Opal
7 a.m.	Chrysolite		7 p.m.	Sardonyx
8 a.m.	Amethyst		8 p.m.	Chalcedony
9 a.m.	Kunzite		9 p.m.	Jade
10 a.m.	Sapphire		10 p.m.	Jasper
11 a.m.	Garnet		11 p.m.	Lodestone
12 noon	Onyx		12 midnight	Diamond

Stones of the Guardian Angels

The guardian angels that preside over the 12 months of the year and the 12 signs of the zodiac (according to Agrippa) are listed in the following chart, along with the sacred talismanic stone ascribed to them. If, according to the modern groupings, your zodiacal sign falls in a different month than that listed, you should choose the guardian angel and corresponding stone to which you feel most drawn. For example, if you are a *January* Capricorn, you may feel a stronger connection to either Gabriel and the onyx (for January) or to Humiel and the beryl (for Capricorn).

Month	Zodiacal Sign	Guardian Angel	Talismanic Stone
January	Aquarius	Gabriel	Onyx
February	Pisces	Barchiel	Jasper
March	Aries	Malchediel	Ruby
April	Taurus	Asmodal	Topaz
May	Gemini	Ambriel	Carbuncle (Garnet)
June	Cancer	Muriel	Emerald
July	Leo	Herchel	Sapphire
August	Virgo	Humatiel	Diamond
September	Libra	Zuriel	Jacinth
October	Scorpio	Barbiel	Agate
November	Sagittarius	Adnachiel	Amethyst
December	Capricorn	Humiel	Beryl

Birthstones of the Chinese Zodiac

The gemstones that correspond to the Chinese Zodiac are as follow:

Year of the:	Gemstone
Rat	Emerald
Ox	Lapis Lazuli
Tiger	Ruby
Cat (or Rabbit)	Sapphire
Dragon	Ruby
Snake	Opal
Horse	Topaz
Goat	Sapphire
Monkey	Tiger's Eye
Rooster	Topaz
Dog	Ruby
Pig (or Boar)	Moonstone

To find your Chinese zodiac sign, use the chart on the following pages to see which animal corresponds with the date of your birth.

Date Range	Animal	Date Range	Animal
2/5/24–1/23/25	Rat	2/10/48–1/28/49	Rat
1/24/25–2/12/26	Ox	1/29/49–2/16/50	Ox
2/13/26–2/1/27	Tiger	2/17/50–2/5/51	Tiger
2/2/27–1/22/28	Cat	2/6/51–1/26/52	Cat
1/23/28–2/9/29	Dragon	1/27/52–2/13/53	Dragon
2/10/29–1/29/30	Snake	2/14/53–2/2/54	Snake
1/30/30–2/16/31	Horse	2/3/54–1/23/55	Horse
2/17/31–2/5/32	Goat	1/24/55–2/11/56	Goat
2/6/32–2/25/33	Monkey	2/12/56–1/30/57	Monkey
1/26/33–2/13/34	Rooster	1/31/57–2/17/58	Rooster
2/14/34–2/3/35	Dog	2/18/58–2/7/59	Dog
2/4/35–1/23/36	Pig	2/8/59–1/27/60	Pig
1/24/36–2/10/37	Rat	1/28/60–2/14/61	Rat
2/11/37–1/30/38	Ox	2/15/61–2/4/62	Ox
1/31/38–2/18/38	Tiger	2/5/62–1/24/63	Tiger
2/19/39–2/7/40	Cat	1/25/63–2/12/64	Cat
2/8/40–1/26/41	Dragon	2/13/64–2/1/65	Dragon
1/27/41–2/14/42	Snake	2/2/65–1/20/66	Snake
2/15/42–2/4/43	Horse	1/21/66–2/8/67	Horse
2/5/43–1/24/44	Goat	2/9/67–1/29/68	Goat
1/25/44–2/12/45	Monkey	1/30/68–2/16/69	Monkey
2/13/45–2/1/46	Rooster	2/17/69–2/5/70	Rooster
2/2/46–1/21/47	Dog	2/6/70–1/26/71	Dog
1/22/47–2/9/48	Pig	1/27/74–2/10/75	Pig

Date Range	Animal	Date Range	Animal
2/15/72–2/2/73	Rat	2/19/96–2/6/97	Rat
2/3/73–1/22/74	Ox	2/7/97–1/27/98	Ox
1/23/74–2/10/75	Tiger	1/28/98–2/15/99	Tiger
2/11/75–1/30/76	Cat	2/16/99–2/4/00	Cat
1/31/76–2/17/77	Dragon	2/5/00–1/23/01	Dragon
2/18/77–2/6/78	Snake	1/24/01–2/11/02	Snake
2/7/78–1/27/79	Horse	2/12/02–1/31/03	Horse
1/28/79–2/15/80	Goat	2/1/03–1/21/04	Goat
2/16/80–2/4/81	Monkey	1/22/04–2/8/05	Monkey
2/5/81–1/24/82	Rooster	2/9/05–1/28/06	Rooster
1/25/82–2/12/83	Dog	1/29/06–2/17/07	Dog
2/13/83–2/1/84	Pig	2/18/07–2/6/08	Pig
2/2/84–2/19/85	Rat		
2/20/85–2/8/86	Ox		
2/9/86–1/28/87	Tiger		
1/29/87–2/16/88	Cat		
2/17/88–2/5/89	Dragon		
2/6/89–1/26/90	Snake		
1/27/90–2/14/91	Horse		
2/15/91–2/3/92	Goat		
2/4/92–1/22/93	Monkey		
1/23/93–2/9/94	Rooster		
2/10/94–1/30/95	Dog		
1/31/95–2/18/96	Pig		

Daily Stones for Protection

The corresponding stones, when worn on the days listed, are said to protect their wearer from harm.

Sunday	Diamond, Pearl, Sunstone, Topaz
Monday	Emerald, Moonstone, Quartz Crystal
Tuesday	Emerald, Star Sapphire, Topaz
Wednesday	Amethyst, Lodestone, Star Ruby, Turquoise
Thursday	Carnelian, Cat's Eye, Sapphire
Friday	Cat's Eye, Emerald, Ruby
Saturday	Amethyst, Diamond, Labradorite, Turquoise

Daily Stones for Good Luck

Wearing a stone from the following chart on the appropriate day of the week, is purported to bring good luck.

Sunday	Ruby
Monday	Moonstone
Tuesday	Coral (Pink or White)
Wednesday	Emerald
Thursday	Cat's Eye
Friday	Diamond
Saturday	Sapphire

Gemstones of the Four Seasons

Traditionally, each of the four seasons is symbolized by a different gemstone. Some people believe that wearing a gemstone during its corresponding season will bring them good luck.

Spring	Emerald
Summer	Ruby
Autumn	Sapphire
Winter	Diamond

Traditional Stones and Precious Metals for Wedding Anniversaries

1st	Gold	**16th**	Peridot
2nd	Garnet	**17th**	(Watches)
3rd	Pearl	**18th**	Cat's Eye
4th	Blue Topaz	**19th**	Aquamarine
5th	Sapphire	**20th**	Emerald
6th	Amethyst	**25th**	Silver
7th	Onyx	**30th**	Pearl
8th	Tourmaline	**35th**	Emerald
9th	Lapis Lazuli	**40th**	Ruby
10th	Diamond	**45th**	Sapphire
11th	Turquoise	**50th**	Gold
12th	Jade	**55th**	Alexandrite
13th	Citrine	**60th**	Diamond
14th	Opal	**70th**	Sapphire
15th	Ruby	**80th**	Ruby

Lucky Birth Stones
"A Time-Honored Rhyme"
(From *The Occult and Curative Powers of Precious Stones*, by William Thomas Fernie, M.D.)

By her in January born
No gem save Garnets should be worn;
They will ensure her constancy,
True friendship and fidelity.

The February-born shall find
Sincerity and peace of mind,
Freedom from passion and from care,
If they the Amethyst will wear.

Who in this world of ours, her eyes
In March first opens, shall be wise.
In days of peril, firm and brave,
And wear a Bloodstone to her grave.

She who from April dates her tears,
Diamonds shall wear, lest bitter tears
For vain repentance flow; this stone,
Emblem for innocence is known.

Who first beholds the light of day,
In spring's sweet flowery month of May,
And wears an Emerald all her life,
Shall be a loved and happy wife.

Who comes with summer to this Earth,
And owes to June her hour of birth,
With ring of Agate on her hand,
Can health, wealth, and long life command.

The glowing Ruby shall adorn
Those who in warm July are born;
Then will they be exempt and free
From love's doubt and anxiety.

Wear Sardonyx, or for thee
No conjugal felicity;
The August-born without this stone,
Tis said, must live unloved and lone.

A maiden born when autumn leaves
Are rustling in September's breeze
A Sapphire on her brow should bind;
Twill cure diseases of the mind.

October's child is born for woe,
And life's vicissitudes must know;
But lay an Opal on her breast,
And hope will lull those foes to rest.

Who first comes to this world below,
With drear November's fog and snow,
Should prize the Topaz's amber hue,
Emblem of friends and lovers true.

If cold December gives you birth,
The month of snow, and ice, and mirth,
Place on your hand a Turquoise blue;
Success will bless whate'er you do.

Chapter 8

Stone Oracles
and Omens

The art of divination by stones dates back to antiquity and has been practiced in one form or another by Shamans, priests, and occult practitioners from all cultures the world over. Gemstone divination, like most other occult methods of prediction, is a system that "speaks" to the psychic mind. It also takes many forms—ranging from the simple to the highly complex.

Throughout the centuries, many different stones (including both precious and semiprecious varieties) have been employed by persons seeking to obtain knowledge of the future, tap into unseen worlds, and know the will of the gods.

> *"Divination is both art and skill, and a Witch's proficiency depends on his or her natural psychic gifts and regular practice."*
>
> —Rosemary Ellen Guiley, *The Encyclopedia of Witches and Witchcraft*

Crystal-gazing

Spheres of crystal have long been favored by individuals who practice the ancient art of crystal-gazing, which is known formally as crystallomancy. However, in his book *The Occult and Curative Powers of Stones*, William T. Fernie, M.D. writes, "All precious stones, when cut with smooth surfaces, and intently gazed upon, are able to produce somnambulism in the same degree as the Crystal, likewise to induce visions (in the same way as hypnotism may be induced by fixing the eyes intently for a time on any shining object near at hand)."

The art of crystal-gazing is one that originated in ancient times and continues to be practiced today. It is a form of scrying, and has long been popular amongst Gypsies and Witches alike.

Seers from centuries past were known to perform elaborate ceremonies prior to consulting a crystal ball. Following a necessary period of fasting, bathing, and prayer, a magick circle would be inscribed upon the floor and within it the seer would stand, facing East. Brandishing such ritual tools as a sword, wand, and compass, the seer would then proceed to recite certain incantations and perform conjurations to call forth spirits.

Crystal balls, according to some occultists, should be used as oracles only during the waxing phase of the moon, and "recharged" by the light of a full moon. They should always be kept covered with a silk cloth when not in use, and never exposed to the rays of the sun, lest their mystical powers be lost.

Crystals, according to Fernie, can be charged more quickly (but not more effectually) by individuals of a "magnetic temperament" (those with dark hair, dark eyes, and a dark complexion) than persons of an "electric temperament" (those with light hair and light to fair skin). And because it was held that purity gave "power in all magnetic and occult experiments," prepubescent males and young virgin females "of unsophisticated mind" were once thought to make the most powerful seers. (This being the reason why, in olden times, it was common for sorcerers to employ young children to do their scrying for them.) Women, particularly widows, were regarded as being second most powerful when it came to the art of scrying, for they were believed to possess unalloyed magnetism "by reason of purity of the amatory functions." However, men, as a rule, "are not so readily developed into Seer-ship as the female," says Fernie, "but they become superlatively powerful, and correct, when so developed."

Among many persons uninitiated into the art of scrying, the crystal ball is erroneously thought of as a mystical device in which images of past, present, or future events are miraculously made to manifest. However, in reality, they do not function in such a fantastic manner. They do not display images like television screens, nor do they radiate with otherworldly powers.

A crystal ball, or whatever object a scryer utilizes as a speculum, works simply as a tool to help a person of clairvoyant ability tap into realms not normally perceived by the five human senses. It is, as Sybil Leek once put it, "an aid to concentration, a focal point to help the normal senses to become subdued so that they do not intrude." When used properly, a crystal ball will stimulate the "sixth sense," enabling visions to manifest in the mind's eye of the person gazing into the crystal.

Often, the visions a seer experiences while crystal scrying are symbolic images (the language of the subconscious mind) and not "psychic news footage of future events" (to quote Scott Cunningham). Crystal scrying may also induce unbidden thoughts—words, phrases, or complete sentences—to manifest within the seer's mind either in conjunction with, or independent of, symbolic or actual images.

> *"My personal observation is that after searching through many forms of fortune telling today, the crystal gazer is the person most likely to have a genuine psychic ability."*

> —Sybil Leek

Lithomancy

Lithomancy—from the Greek *lithos* ("stone" or "rock") and *mancy* ("divination")—is the art and practice of prognosticating the future or interpreting omens by means of casting or scrying stones, including crystals and gems. (Some individuals use the term *lithomancy* when referring to divinatory methods involving pebbles and rocks, and the term *lythomancy* when referring to those that use crystals and semiprecious stones.) It is believed by some to be the most ancient of divinatory methods, and can be traced back to Revelations 21:18 with its powerful astrological/zodiacal connections. It can be used to gain insight to not only the future, but also to the past and the present. When performing divinatory work with certain stones associated with the chakra known as the Third Eye, a person's past incarnations can sometimes be revealed as well.

The practice of lithomancy is said to be most popular among diviners in Europe and the British Isles. However, it has been practiced in many forms by nearly every culture around the world.

It typically employs 13 stones—seven of which are used to represent the sun, the moon, and the planets Mars, Mercury, Jupiter, Saturn, and Venus. The remaining six are used to represent the home, affairs of the heart, health, magick, and news.

For maximum effectiveness, the stones used in a reading should be gathered from nature during favorable astrological configurations and by using one's intuitive powers as a guide. The sizes and shapes of the stones selected should be similar.

A typical lithomantic reading basically involves a given number of the stones aforementioned being randomly drawn from a pouch (or other container), tumbled in the hands like dice while a particular question is asked aloud or concentrated upon, and then tossed onto a circle divided into sections representing different emotions and advice. The question is then answered by interpreting the influence and placement of the stones within the circle. Some lithomancers feel that the stones that land outside of the circle are also significant in a reading.

Another popular method of lithomancy uses three small stones—one to represent an affirmative answer, one to represent a negative answer, and one to serve as an indicator. While concentrating on a yes-or-no question, roll all three of the stones between your hands, as you would dice, and then cast them onto the ground. Whichever stone lands the closest to the indicator determines the answer to your question. If the affirmative and negative stones land within equal distance to the indicator, this usually means that an answer is unavailable at the present time. Try the divination again later, and perhaps rephrase your question.

There are many other ways to divine using stones, whether they are ordinary pebbles, painted stones, stones inscribed with symbols, crystals, or gems. The amount and types of stones used in lithomancy, as well as the actual method, often vary from one lithomancer to the next. There are no right or wrong ways to do it, as a diviner's natural psychic abilities are the key factor in any divination, and how well-developed those abilities are is almost always what determines the accuracy of a reading.

Drawing omens from the way light is reflected off the natural sides or cut facets of a crystal or gemstone placed on a black cloth is another form of lithomancy. When divining stones in this manner, it is not uncommon for some persons with an increased level of psychic sensitivity to also experience visions and/or telepathic messages.

Pessomancy

Pessomancy is the art and practice of divination through the use of pebbles. It is an old and simple mantic art that is believed to have been practiced by both the ancient Greeks and the ancient Egyptians.

Pessomancy is basically performed by shaking a number of pebbles in a basket, bowl, or buffalo horn, and then dumping them out onto the ground or floor. The pessomancer then looks for symbolic messages in the patterns formed by the scattered pebbles in much the same way that a tasseographer (tea-leaf reader) looks for symbolic messages formed by wet tea leaves clinging to the inside of a teacup.

Margaritomancy

Margaritomancy—from the Latin *margarita* ("pearl")—is the art and practice of divination by means of casting pearls or observing a pearl in an oyster.

In ancient times, a form of margaritomancy was used to determine the guilt or innocence of a man or woman suspected of committing a crime. A pearl would be placed inside a cast iron pot, which would then be suspended over a fire. If the pearl began bouncing around or jumped out of the pot when the accused person's name was recited by the local magistrate, this was taken as an irrefutable sign of his or her guilt.

Simple Stone Divinations

Using stones to answer "yes" or "no" to any given question is perhaps the simplest of all divinatory methods known to mankind.

Begin by choosing two stones of equal size and shape—a white one to represent an affirmative reply, and a black one to represent a negative one. After consecrating and charging the stones to work for you as tools of divination, place them into a pouch. Light the wick of a purple candle and gaze into its flame for several minutes while concentrating solely upon a single yes-or-no question. When you feel ready, close your eyes, reach into the pouch, and draw one of the stones. The answer to your question is thus indicated by the color of the randomly chosen stone.

This same method can be employed to determine the sex of an unborn child. Use a moonstone, chalcedony, or quartz crystal (symbolic of the feminine energies associated with the moon) or a pink-colored stone (such as pink tourmaline or rose quartz) to represent a baby girl. Use a sunstone, golden topaz, or tiger's eye (symbolic of the masculine energies associated with the sun) or a blue-colored stone (such as blue tourmaline or turquoise) to represent a baby boy. Before placing the stones into the pouch and drawing one, lay them upon the pregnant woman's belly for several minutes while chanting:

*Let one of these stones reveal to me
the gender of the child to be.*

Hag Stones

Stones having naturally occurring holes through them have been used for many centuries as devices to see ghosts and fairies. Peering through such a stone with one eye shut is said to induce psychic visions. Also known in some parts of the world as "hag stones," holed stones obviously symbolize the female genitals (which strongly link them to fertility magick and the Feminine Divine) and are believed by some people to also possess healing virtues.

In the 18th century, historian Francis Grose wrote: "A Stone with a Hole in it, hung at the Bed's head, will prevent the Night Mare; it is therefore called a Hag Stone, from that disorder which is occasioned by a Hag or Witch sitting on the Stomach of the party afflicted. It also prevents Witches riding Horses: for which purpose it is often tied to a Stable Key."

In her book, *An ABC of Witchcraft Past and Present*, Doreen Valiente attributes the magickal powers of the holed stone to its being "a female emblem, representing the portal of birth."

Crawling or being passed through a hole in a stone has been thought for many a century to bring good luck and be an effective cure for a number of physical ailments, including arthritis, boils, rickets (an infantile disease marked by defective development of bones), scrofula (a tuberculous condition mainly afflicting young children), spinal diseases, and the whooping cough. It has also been used to vanquish a condition of barrenness (an old term for female infertility).

Belief in the magickal and miraculous healing virtues of holed stones can be found in many cultures the world over, and the curious old custom of crawling through them is thought to have originally been a simple Pagan fertility rite.

"To find a stone with a hole in it is a special sign of the favour of Diana."

—Charles Godfrey Leland, author of
Aradia, or the Gospel of the Witches

Rune Stones

Rune stones (divinatory stones upon which ancient Norse and Teutonic alphabet sigils are carved, etched, or painted) gained popularity in the 1980s, although runic symbols date back to the prehistoric Neolithic and Bronze Ages (circa 8000 B.C.–2000 B.C.) Rune stones are typically made from small polished stones of various shapes with smooth rounded edges. They are as popular among Witches as they are among New Age people—a personal opinion based on the fact that most of the Witches whom I've met over the years each own at least one set of rune stones for divination and spiritual guidance.

My own rune stones, which I work with on occasion, were bought many years ago from a quaint Lake Placid gift shop that smelled of potpourri, scented candles, and incense. The set consists of 25 shiny hematite stones that always feel quite cold to the touch. When not in use, I keep them stored in a lovely dark blue drawstring pouch silk-screened with celestial designs and astrological symbols.

Although I personally find myself drawn more strongly to Tarot cards and dowsing pendulums when it comes to divinatory work, I have worked with the rune stones on a number of occasions and usually for the guidance of others. (I seldom ever divine for myself.) By my own experience with the stones, I've found that runecastings performed during the dark of the moon tend to be more accurate than those done during other lunar phases.

Rune stone divination, for the most part, is fairly simple to perform. In most cases, the stones are randomly drawn from a pouch and meditated upon, cast in lots in a fashion similar to the ancient Chinese oracle known as the *I Ching* (Book of Changes), or arranged in crosses and wheels in the same way that fortune-telling cards are laid out in spreads. According to author Rosemary Ellen Guiley, "Like the *I Ching* and Tarot, runes do not provide answers, but provide the means to answers; they are considered keys to self-transformation."

The Mystical Moonstone

The moonstone has long been regarded as a stone of clairvoyance and prophetic dreams. Many people believe that it works best for divination when the moon is increasing, for this is the time of the month when the moonstone's power is said to be at its greatest. Other occult practitioners, however, are of the opposite opinion and feel that the waning moon is a more appropriate time for divining with moonstone.

According to an old grimoire, if a moonstone is placed under the tongue on the first and 10th day of the new moon, it can enable a person to see into the future. Similarly, romantic legend holds that if an unmarried woman holds a moonstone to her lips beneath the rays of a full moon, she will receive a vision of her future husband. And if lovers wish to read the future of their relationship, a moonstone placed in the mouth when the moon is full will reveal it, whether good or grim.

Occult practitioners of old believed that other gems could endow an individual with the power to prophesy things yet to come by being placed under the tongue as well. Stones possessing such attributes include the tiger's eye, emerald, and mother-of-pearl (when used on the first or 29th day of the lunar month).

"Moonstone beads or pendants are worn during divinatory acts and produce psychicsm in general."

—Scott Cunningham

Stones of Divination and Psychism

Not only can gemstones be utilized as powerful divinatory tools as shown by the previous examples, they can also be used as a means to awaken one's clairvoyant abilities, strengthen the psychic mind, and help sharpen intuitive powers.

In her reference book describing the metaphysical properties of the mineral kingdom, Melody mentions several stones that are beneficial to diviners. One of them, mosandrite, is said to possess the power to "stimulate the gift of prophecy and supplement the skills necessary for divination." Another, the Andean opal, facilitates divination, while lamprophyllite provides "insight to prophetic questions."

Some of the many ways in which gemstones are used to facilitate divinatory abilities include the wearing of gems in the form of amuletic jewelry, the carrying of stones in a mojo bag, the placing of certain stones upon the Third Eye chakra, and the drinking of special gemstone elixirs and waters. Some individuals find that, when performed on a daily basis, the act of meditating upon a particular stone while holding it improves their abilities to divine.

"Wearing psychic-influencing stones such as lapis lazuli, moonstone, azurite or others may help you tap into your psychic awareness," says Scott Cunningham. In his book *Cunningham's Encyclopedia of Crystal, Gem and Metal Magic*, he dedicates a short chapter to stone divination, referring to it as "an excellent form of this ancient art." His advice to those seeking help in decision-making or desiring to gain a glimpse of events yet to unfurl, is simply, "look to the stones for help."

The following types of stones are examples of those associated with divination and psychism: amethyst, aquamarine, azurite, beryl, citrine, emerald, flint, hematite, holey stones, jet, lapis lazuli, mica, moonstone, obsidian, quartz crystal, and tiger's eye.

Gemstones of the Major Arcana

Each of the 22 symbols of the Major Arcana has one or more corresponding gemstones, which can be used instead of Tarot cards in a divinatory reading (see pages 141–142).

To perform a Tarot reading using stones instead of cards, place the 22 stones representing the Major Arcana in a cauldron. With your eyes shut, concentrate on your question or problem and randomly draw one of the stones from the cauldron. Open your eyes and gaze upon the stone. Use your psychic mind to interpret its meaning.

For a more in-depth reading, draw three stones from the cauldron—one to represent the past, one to represent the present, and one to represent the future.

The ancient Celtic method (also known as the Celtic Cross) is perhaps the most popular of Tarot card layouts. To perform a stone reading using this method, randomly draw 10 stones from the cauldron while concentrating on a question, visualizing a goal, or making a wish.

The 1st stone represents the influence that is affecting either the querent or the matter of inquiry. Place it at the center of the layout.

Place the 2nd stone on top of the 1st one. This stone represents the obstacles and opposing forces affecting the Querent.

Place the 3rd stone to the North of (directly above) the two center stones to represent the Querent's aim or ideal in the matter.

Place the 4th stone to the South of (directly below) the two center stones to represent the foundation or basis of the matter.

Place the 5th stone to the West (left) of the two center stones to represent the recent past.

Place the 6th stone to the East (right) of the two center stones to represent the immediate future.

To the right of the 6th stone, lay the 7th through the 10th stones one by one into a straight line upwards, with the 10th stone at the top.

The 7th stone represents the querent; the 8th stone represents his or her environment; the 9th stone represents what is feared or hoped for; and the 10th stone represents the final outcome that is brought about by the influences of the other stones in the reading.

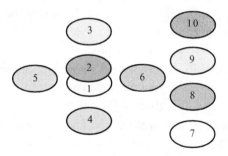

Celtic Cross Gemstone Tarot Spread

The following tables contain the 22 symbols of the Rider-Waite Major Arcana, along with their basic divinatory meanings and corresponding gemstones based on traditional planetary/Elemental correspondences. (Stone correspondences according to Scott Cunningham's popular "Stone Tarot" are also included.)

Major Arcana Gemstone Correspondences			
Card	*Divinatory Meaning*	*Gemstone*	*Cunningham*
Fool (0)	Folly, vanity, imbalance extravagance, or intoxication.	Aventurine or Topaz	Agate
Magician (1)	Magickal attainment, control, skill, self-confidence, creative powers, or will.	Agate or Opal	Quartz Crystal
High Priestess (2)	Wisdom, spirituality, secrets, female mysteries, or hidden influences at work.	Moonstone	Emerald or Pearl
Empress (3)	Receptive energy, femininity, money, marriage, fertility, or childbirth.	Emerald or Turquoise	Olivine, Peridot, or Turquoise
Emperor (4)	Projective energy, masculinity, stability, authority, leadership, or position of power.	Bloodstone or Diamond	Ruby
Hierophant (5)	Conformity, need for social approval, religious matters, a teacher or employer.	Jade or Topaz	Topaz
Lovers (6)	Platonic or erotic love, choice, attraction, or temptation.	Alexandrite or Iceland Spar	Rose Quartz
Chariot (7)	Triumph or vengeance.	Amber	Staurolite
Strength, or Fortitude (8)	Courage or physical strength.	Jasper or Lapis Lazuli	Diamond or Garnet
Hermit (9)	Silent council, help offered, mysticism, enlightenment, seclusion, or prudence.	Peridot	Blue Tourmaline or Sapphire
Wheel of Fortune (10)	Chance, destiny, good or bad luck.	Amethyst	Black Opal or Sardonyx

Major Arcana Gemstone Correspondences *(cont'd)*

Card	Divinatory Meaning	Gemstone	Cunningham
Justice (11)	Justice served, balance, success in lawsuits and legal matters.	Cat's Eye	Carnelian
Hanged Man (12)	Sacrafice, trials, or suspension.	Beryl or Chrysocolla	Aquamarine or Beryl
Death (13)	Transformation, destruction followed by renewal, mortality, new opportunities, or change.	Bloodstone or Snakestone	Amber
Temperance (14)	Moderation, self-control, or successful combinations.	Amethyst or Jacinth	Amethyst
Devil (15)	Violence, evil, depression, physical or mental illness.	Black Diamond, Jet, or Obsidian	Any square, black stone
Tower (16)	Unforseen catastrophe, conflict, misery, or ruin.	Ruby	Lava Rock or Lodestone
Star (17)	Hope, bright prospects, inspiration, wishes granted, or good health.	Chalcedony or Zircon	Meteorite or any star stone
Moon (18)	Deception, hidden enemies, occult forces, psychic powers, intuition, or female troubles.	Pearl or White Coral	Chalcedony or Moonstone
Sun (19)	Happiness, contentment, attainment of goals, or achievements.	Chrysoleth	Sunstone or Tiger's Eye
Judgement (20)	Awakening, renewal, outcome, or change of position.	Fire Opal or Hematite	Fossil
World (21)	Completion, success in all undertakings, travel, or a change in residence.	Onyx	Kunzite or Opal

Gemstone Dream Divination

The art and practice of interpreting dreams to foretell the future and reveal the unknown is one of the oldest methods of divination known to mankind. Formally known as *oneiromancy* (Greek for "divination by dreams"), it is also one of the most popular methods—especially among Witches and other practitioners of the magickal and divinatory arts.

The following gemstone-related dream interpretations are based on those found in Gustavus Hindman Miller's *10,000 Dreams Interpreted*, which was originally published at the beginning of the last century.

Agate

To dream about an agate is said to indicate a minor advancement where business affairs are concerned. However, to dream about losing or being robbed of an agate warns of demotions or setbacks in the workplace.

Amethyst

To dream about an amethyst indicates "contentment with fair business," according to author Gustavus Hindman Miller. However, if a young woman should dream about losing an amethyst, this is said to indicate a "broken engagement and slights in love."

Bloodstone

To dream about a bloodstone is said to indicate misfortune in one's undertakings. To dream that a bloodstone is given to you as a gift indicates that you are soon to lose a friend, but, as a result, will gain another who will prove to be more worthy of your friendship.

Diamond

To dream about owning a diamond is said to be an indication that you will be the recipient of great honor and recognition from high places. To dream about receiving a diamond as a gift from your lover portends a blissful marital union. However, it is said to be an omen of extreme bad luck, disgrace, or death for one to dream about losing a diamond. To dream about stealing diamonds from the dead indicates that your disloyalty to a friend will be discovered. To dream that a rhinestone changes into a diamond is a sign that unexpected good fortune will arise from some insignificant act on the part of the dreamer.

Emerald

To dream about an emerald indicates the inheritance of property, but, at the same time, warns of trouble. To dream about purchasing an emerald is said to portend "unfortunate dealings." When a man dreams that he sees his fiancé wearing one or more emeralds, this is usually a warning that he will soon be spurned for a wealthier suitor.

Pearl

To dream about pearls is an indication of happiness, good fortune, success in business matters, or an engagement. However, according to Miller, "indescribable sadness and sorrow through bereavement or misunderstandings" are portended by dreams in which pearls are broken or lost.

Ruby

To dream about a ruby indicates good luck in either business ventures or affairs of the heart. However, if a woman should dream about losing a ruby, this is said to be a warning of "the approaching indifference of her lover."

Sapphire

To dream about a sapphire is said to indicate a "fortunate gain" for the dreamer. If a woman should have a dream about this gem, this is said to be an indication that she has chosen her lover wisely.

Sardonyx

To dream about a sardonyx indicates an increase of one's material possessions and, in some cases, the overcoming of poverty. However, to dream about losing or discarding a sardonyx is said to be a warning to the dreamer that opportunities for improvement might be overlooked.

Topaz

To dream about topaz is an indication of good fortune and "very pleasing companions." To dream about receiving any type of topaz jewelry from someone other than a family member indicates an involvement in a love affair. According to Miller, if a woman should dream about losing topaz jewelry, this is a warning of "jealous friends who court her position."

Turquoise

To dream about turquoise indicates that one or more of your desires will soon be realized. If a woman should dream that any type of turquoise jewelry has been stolen from her, this portends that she will be unlucky in love.

Chapter 9

Cursed Stones

The Curse of the Hope Diamond

It is said, "diamonds are forever." But as the strange history of the infamous Hope diamond would seem to indicate, some ancient curses can be just as everlasting.

The Hope diamond (named after Henry Philip Hope, who acquired it in the 19th century) is a billion-year-old, flawless, dark blue diamond. Weighing in at 45.52 carats, it is the world's largest deep blue diamond. It is said to have originally been slightly more than 112 carats, but was cut down at least twice in the past three centuries.

This exquisite jewel is extremely rare, for unlike most other blue diamonds that normally phosphoresce light blue when exposed to ultraviolet light, the Hope diamond phosphoresces red. And even further setting it apart from other diamonds is the very fact that it is without question the most famous of all precious stones reputed to carry with it a curse that brings great misfortune to whomever owns or wears it.

Legend has it that the curse of the Hope diamond began in the 17th century with a French jewel trader by the name of Jean-Baptiste Tavernier. While visiting India, he allegedly purchased this priceless jewel from a thief who had broken into a sacred temple and stolen it from the forehead or eye socket of a gold statue of Sita—a powerful six-armed Hindu deity worshipped as the divine consort of the god Vishnu and revered as an incarnation of the goddess Lakshmi. (According to a slightly different version of the legend, it was Tavernier, himself, who stole the precious jewel from the idol.)

In the year 1668, after smuggling the diamond to Paris, Tavernier sold it to King Louis XIV of France and was made a noble. However, his seemingly good fortune took a fatal turn when, while traveling in Russia, he was brutally torn to pieces by a rabid pack of wild dogs. Tavernier died from the attack—the victim, some would say, of the curse placed on the diamond by an angry goddess.

However, the evil curse of the blue diamond was not to be lifted by Tavernier's death. The beautiful jewel, which was now known as the "French Blue," would claim many other unfortunate souls in the centuries to follow, causing some of its owners to lose their fortunes, their health, their sanity, and, in some instances, even their lives.

King Louis had the diamond cut into the shape of a heart and presented it to his mistress, Marquise de Montespan, as a token of his affection for her. Soon after, she was arrested on the charges of practicing sorcery and attending a Satanic Black Mass at which a number of children had been ritually sacrificed, their blood drained into chalices and mixed with flour to make the host. It is said that during the diabolical ritual the King's mistress willingly allowed her naked body to be used as an altar.

The scandal that this unleashed caused Marquise de Montespan to lose favor with the King, who ordered her to return the "French Blue" to prevent "the stigma of her crimes" from being attached to it. After the jewel was once again in his possession, he developed gangrene and suffered an agonizing death in 1715.

King Louis XVI, who inherited the large ornate diamond and wore it for special ceremonial occasions, is also believed by many to have fallen victim to its curse. By the year 1789 his country had plunged into bankruptcy and the French Revolution was underway. After the monarchy was overthrown on August 10, 1792, the King attempted to flee to Austria with his wife, Marie Antionette, but they were captured and returned to Paris. In January of 1793, the royal couple was sent to the guillotine for the crime of treason.

The Princess de Lamballe (Marie Antionette's closest friend and confidant) is said to have borrowed the blue diamond from the Queen on at least one occasion, and she too met with a violent death. On September 3, 1792, for her refusal to take an oath against the monarchy, she was thrown to an angry mob that savagely raped and beat her before cutting off her head and mounting it on a spike outside the window of the cell where Marie Antionette was imprisoned. Her headless body was then torn to pieces, which were also placed atop spikes and gruesomely displayed throughout the town.

The blue diamond, along with the rest of the crown jewels, had been confiscated from the King and Queen long before their bloody executions were carried out, and it was put on public display in Paris at a repository called the *Garde Meuble*. But the building apparently was not secure enough, for it was pillaged in September of 1791 by a gang of thieving rogues, who made off with the jewels.

The blue diamond resurfaced in London around the year 1813 and Wilhelm Fals, a Dutch jeweler and diamond cutter, was commissioned to recut the diamond to its present size. (Some claim this was done in an attempt to conceal the diamond's true origin.) The curse of the diamond apparently struck again when Fals was later robbed and murdered by his son, Hendrik. Many years later, Hendrik Fals, guilty with the blood of his father upon his hands, committed suicide.

The diamond made its way into the hands of a jeweler named Daniel Eliason, who purchased it in 1823 and then sold it to King George IV of England, unleashing more misfortune. The king was forced to marry his cousin, Caroline of Brunswick—a woman whom he detested and denied queenship to. Their ill-fated marriage ended in separation less than a year later and George was made to endure public ridicule and scandal. His daughter, Princess Charlotte, died at childbirth, and he became addicted to both alcohol and laudanum (a mixture of alcohol and opium derivatives). He became reclusive and eventually went mad, meeting with death in 1830 after a series of strokes brought on a hemorrhage in his stomach. After the death of King George IV, the diamond was sold to pay off the many debts that his extravagant spending and indulgent lifestyle had incurred.

That same year, Henry Philip Hope (of the wealthy European banking family that helped finance the Louisiana Purchase) bought the diamond for a sum of £18000, and, from then on, it became known as the Hope diamond. It remained in the private collection of the Hope family for three generations before being sold in 1901 to an American jeweler by Lord Francis Hope, who had gambled his way to bankruptcy and suffered scandal and an unhappy marriage. His wife, an American actress named May Yohe, claimed that the diamond was evil and prophesied that it would bring misfortune to all who owned it. So strong was her belief in the diamond's curse that she even wrote about it in a book called *The Mystery of the Hope Diamond*. She eventually left Lord Francis Hope for another man and died in poverty in 1913.

It is unknown whether the New York jeweler, Simon Frankel, was affected by the alleged curse, however, he sold the Hope diamond to its next owner and victim—a French broker by the name of Jacques Colot. Colot is said to have gone insane and committed suicide shortly after selling the diamond to Prince Ivan Kanitovski, a Russian nobleman.

Kanitovski supposedly gave (or lent) the blue diamond to his lover, a young and beautiful Folies Bergere actress named Loren Ladue. On the first night that she wore it, he shot her to death. Shortly after, Russian revolutionaries stabbed him to death in the street.

The diamond was then purchased by a Greek jewel broker who paid little or no heed to its cursed history. He later drove his automobile over a cliff, killing himself, his wife, and their child. To this very day, some wonder whether the tragedy was a mere accident, a suicide, or the result of foul play. But one thing is certain, and that is the connection that existed between the victims and the Hope diamond.

A Persian diamond merchant named Habib Bey owned the diamond for a short length of time before meeting with an untimely death when the French steamer, on which he was a passenger, sank.

For the reported sum of $400,000, the Hope diamond became the prized possession of Turkish sultan, Abdul Hamid II, in 1908. He was soon to become known as "Abdul the Damned"—not surprisingly, as all who came into contact with the infamous jewel were met with a cruel fate. Zubayda, the sultan's favorite concubine, wore the diamond and was later murdered by the blade of a dagger. Abu Sabir, one of the sultan's servants, was imprisoned and tortured to death shortly after polishing the diamond for the sultan. Kulub Bey, whose job it was to guard the diamond, was assaulted by a Turkish mob and hanged to death. Jehver Agha, an official of the sultan's treasury, tried to make off with the diamond but was caught and hanged. And one year after having purchased the diamond, the sultan lost the Ottoman Empire when an army revolt toppled him from his throne. It is said that after his deposition he went mad.

Evalyn Walsh McLean (the wife of *Washington Post* proprietor, Edward Beale McLean) was the last private owner of the Hope diamond. She was well aware of the diamond's ominous reputation when she purchased it in 1911 from jeweler Pierre Cartier. However, she was undaunted by it and, oddly enough, even referred to it as her "lucky charm." But shortly after purchasing the diamond, two servants in the McLean household died. Evalyn's 9-year-old son was killed when struck by a car, and her 25-year-old daughter (who had worn the blue diamond at her wedding) took her own life by ingesting a fatal amount of sleeping pills. Edward had an affair with another woman, dissipated their fortune, developed brain atrophy as a result of his chronic addiction to alcohol, and spent the remainder of his days confined to a mental institution. Evalyn was forced to sell the family newspaper and became addicted to morphine. After her death in 1947, her so-called lucky charm was put up for sale to settle the debts of her estate.

Harry Winston, a New York jeweler, purchased the Hope diamond for a sum rumored to be $1 million. He then surprised the nation by donating it to the Smithsonian Institution in 1958, where it was to be the focal point of a newly established collection of gems. At the time, many people were (and continue to be) of the opinion that Winston's donation of the jewel was not merely an act of generosity. They believed it to be his attempt to rid himself of the diamond's evil curse.

But the story of the Hope diamond and its curse (whether real or imagined) does not end there. James Todd, the postal carrier who delivered the diamond to the Smithsonian is said to have experienced a terrible streak of bad luck after handling the package containing the diamond. (Curiously, the million-dollar Hope diamond was shipped via ordinary parcel post!) He suffered a crushed leg in a truck accident, sustained injuries to his head in an automobile accident, and then had the misfortune of having his home burn to the ground.

The Hope diamond is currently housed in the National Museum of Natural History in Washington, DC, where it is on public display in the Janet Annenberg Hooker Hall of Geology, Gems, and Minerals. Many people to this day believe that the beautiful blue gem is responsible for nearly every economic, natural, and political disaster that has befallen the United States since 1958.

As a Witch and a believer in the power of magick and curses, it seems rather odd to me that with so much tragedy seemingly connected to the Hope diamond, there is absolutely no documentation of any sort to indicate that any of its past owners ever made an attempt in any way to have the diamond cleansed of its curse. Perhaps if they had, many lives would have been spared and much tragedy avoided.

[Sources: Marian Fowler, *Hope: Adventures of a Diamond*. Random House Canada, 2002. Ernst A. and Jean Heiniger, *Great Book of Jewels*. 1974.]

Mountain of Light, Curse of Darkness

"He who owns this diamond shall own the world, but he shall also know all its misfortunes. Only God or a woman can wear it with immunity." This is the curse said to be laid upon the beautiful pink Koh-i-Noor diamond by Guru Gobind Singh, who declared that any man who dared to remove the jewel from its original hiding place would be doomed to suffer untold miseries.

The Koh-i-Noor curse is said to be extremely potent. It has been blamed for assassinations and the fall of two empires, and some believe that it can endure for generations. Despite the diamond's grim reputation, people throughout India once believed that water in which this gem was dipped was made fortified with miraculous healing powers.

The infamous Koh-i-Noor diamond is one of the largest diamonds in the world, weighing in at just less than 109 carats.

Its name is Persian for "mountain of light," and its history can be traced back at least 700 years.

According to the writings of Babur, the founder of the Mogul Empire, the diamond was part of the treasure won by Ala-ud-deen (Aladdin) at the conquest of Malwah in the year 1304 A.D.

An old Hindu legend claims that the diamond once belonged to the great god Krishna but was stolen from his possession one night while he was sound asleep. When he awoke to find his beloved jewel missing, he proclaimed a mighty curse upon the diamond and all men who would ever dare to wear it. Women, however, were spared from the curse. From that day forward, many male possessors of the diamond have been met by financial ruin, torture, imprisonment, and death by murder or suicide.

The long and impressive list of men alleged to have fallen victim to the Koh-i-Noor curse includes Nadir, the Shah of Persia, who was assassinated by the captain of his guard during a palace revolt in the year 1747. His successor, Adil, inherited both the diamond and its curse. He was dethroned and blinded by his own brother. Ranjit Singh, the Maharaja of Punjab, also owned the diamond and met with death soon after his acquisition of it. His son, Dalip Singh, lost his kingdom, was exiled, and died impoverished in Paris. All eight of the Maharaja's grandchildren died without heirs.

The Koh-i-Noor diamond made its way to England in 1850 and was presented to Queen Victoria, who originally wore it in a brooch. It was later set in the state crown and worn by Queen Alexandra and Queen Mary. In 1937, Queen Elizabeth wore it for her coronation. Currently, it is housed in the Tower of London along with the rest of the British crown jewels.

Some people in England are of the opinion that the diamond's evil power controls the fate of the Windsor family. Others regard its ancient curse as nothing more than mere superstitious nonsense and view the misfortunes suffered by some of the diamond's previous owners as mere coincidence. Curiously, no male member of the royal family has ever worn the Koh-i-Noor diamond. Perhaps they feel it is far better to be safe than sorry.

[Sources: *www.williamsdiamond.com/famousdiamonds.html*,
www.jewelryexpert.com/articles/Koh-i-noor-Diamond.htm,
www.bbc.co.uk/dna/h2g2/alabaster/A730801,
and *brysonburke.com/lore_kohinoor.html*]

Curses and Ways to Break Them

Many psychics and magickally inclined individuals believe that crystals and gemstones are highly sensitive to the thought vibrations given off by the human mind. If such a thing is indeed fact, then a stone such as the Hope diamond could very well be made into a cursed object simply by projecting that sort of intent into it. Furthermore, the strong emotions of the persons who come into contact with it and suffer the effects of its curse are then absorbed into the stone, strengthening and amplifying the negative energy of the curse even more. Therefore, the more misfortune that it propagates, the stronger the power of the curse grows.

But even if an object such as a stone or a piece of jewelry has never had a curse formally proclaimed upon it, there is enough evidence to substantiate that if enough people strongly believe it to be cursed or a jinx, the object will eventually begin to absorb, and become charged by, the energy of the negative thoughts being projected into it and respond accordingly.

Many experts in the field of the occult claim that in order to break a curse like the ones believed by many to be attached to the Hope and the Koh-i-Noor diamonds, the cursed object must be ritually exorcised and blessed by a person (such as a priest or priestess) gifted with the power to perform such feats.

Another method of curse removal is to have the person that originally laid the curse lift it from the object. However, in the case of the Hope diamond and other jewels bearing centuries-old curses, such a thing is usually not performable unless a strong contact can be established with the deceased person's spirit, and only then if the conjured spirit is willing and able to lift the curse.

Transferring the curse or bad luck to another object (or person, in some cases) by certain magickal applications is another method for dealing with curses and jinxes. It is one that has been employed by many cultures and dates back to primitive times. Although it can be quite an effective method, from a Neo-Pagan point of view it is probably the least ethical.

But when all else fails, the destruction of the cursed object (usually by the cleansing Element of Fire) is often the only way to ever be completely rid of its curse.

Chapter 10

The Lore
of Gemstones

"It is easy to dismiss superstition as absurd, but only those who can break a mirror without a second thought are fully entitled to do so."

—*Strange Stories, Amazing Facts*

Agate

In medieval times it was thought that placing an agate in one's mouth could relieve thirst. It was also believed that drinking water from a chalice or cup containing a ring with a green agate setting could cure barrenness (the inability to have children) in women. Red agate was reputed to hold the power to halt storms and prevent venomous creatures (scorpions, snakes, insects, and the like) from inflicting their bites and stings upon any person who carried or wore the stone.

Amethyst

The ancient Greeks believed that wearing an amethyst acted as a preservative against intoxication. (It is no accident that the word "amethyst" derives from the Greek *a-* ("negative") and *methein* ("to be drunken").

Beryl

Once carried by sailors and fishermen to prevent storms at sea, the beryl was also used, ironically, by Shamans to produce downpours of rain. It was also once believed to keep those who wore it guarded against drowning. The famous "crystal egg," used as a scrying tool by John Dee (the royal magician to Queen Elizabeth I), was actually made of beryl and not clear quartz crystal, as many people wrongly assume. Beryl is known as "the stone of the seer" and its popularity as a gazing speculum at one time surpassed that of quartz crystals.

Bloodstone

The ancient Egyptians believed that the bloodstone possessed the power to open locked doors as well as to topple walls of stone, and many farmers in the Middle Ages were convinced that wearing a bloodstone during the planting of crops ensured a bountiful harvest. However, bloodstone is perhaps best known the world over for its alleged ability to control bleeding when placed upon wounds. Many individuals in the New Age movement also believe that it can be used to cure diseases associated with the blood, such as anemia.

Carnelian

It was once believed that wearing carnelian offered protection against collapsing buildings or falling walls (which undoubtedly made it a popular stone in many earthquake-prone parts of the world). The other virtues of this stone include the ability to still anger, cure bashfulness, dispel depression, and strengthen one's memory. Wearing carnelian is also reputed to ward off lightning and storms, and prevent others from being able to read your thoughts.

Cat's Eye

A gemstone with reflections similar to those from the eye of a cat, the cat's eye was once believed by the Assyrians to possess the power to make a man invisible. In addition, this stone is said to prevent madness, and many New Age healers use it to treat various ailments of the eyes.

Chrysoprase

It was once believed that wearing or carrying a piece of chrysoprase (an apple-green type of chalcedony) gave strength to the eyes, promoted eloquence, stimulated an increase in fertility, and brought relief to those suffering from rheumatism. This stone is also credited with the ability to mend broken hearts.

Coal

Tossing a lump of coal over the left shoulder or carrying it in one's pocket was once thought to bring good luck, while dreaming about coal was said to portend wealth. In England, it was once a common custom for families to place a piece coal in the Christmas stocking for good luck in the coming year.

Coral

At one time it was common for women in Italy to wear a piece of red coral near their private area to regulate the flow of their menses. It is said that, during menstruation, the color of the coral would become pale and return to its normal bright color after the menstrual cycle was over. In his *Encyclopedia of Crystal, Gem and Metal Magic*, Scott Cunningham suggests the idea that coral might have been employed by women for period prediction, and adds, "Coral used for these purposes was carefully hidden from the eyes of men, for, if seen by them, it lost all its magic power."

Crystals

See *Quartz Crystal*.

Diamond

According to Cunningham's *Encyclopedia of Crystal, Gem, and Metal Magic*, it was once a commonly held belief in India that if a woman wore "an unblemished white diamond with a slightly black hue," she would give birth to a child of the male gender. Many people regard the diamond as a good luck stone, while some superstitious folks say that only diamonds faceted into a six-sided cut are lucky. Other people see nothing lucky about the diamond and consider it to be magnet for sorrow and misfortune. In his book, *On Gems and Colors*, magician Jerome Cardan warned readers that the brilliance of the diamond was irritating to the soul in much the same manner that the direct rays of the sun were irritating to the eyes.

Much has been written about the alleged healing powers of the diamond. According to some occult authors, so great is this stone's power to heal that it is able to counteract poisons and cure a plethora of diseases and conditions, including infertility, sexual dysfunction, insomnia, physical weakness, and mental illness. The diamond has long been believed to ensure fidelity and reconcile quarreling lovers—a superstition that no doubt plays a major role in making the diamond the most popular stone for wedding rings. The diamond, according to

Scott Cunningham, "has a wide and varied magical repertoire." Some practitioners of gemstone sorcery, however, are of the opinion that only diamonds received as gifts have any real power to work magick. The ones that are purchased—regardless how beautiful or expensive they might be—have little or no magickal value.

> *"Because diamonds were sacred to the supreme Goddess, they were taken over by the cult of the Virgin; and because of this association with virginity they came to be considered appropriate betrothal gifts."*
>
> —Barbara G. Walker, *The Women's Encyclopedia of Myths and Secrets*

Emerald

Gemstone lore holds that placing an emerald underneath the tongue can give a person knowledge of all things past, present, and future. Known as the "stone of truth," the emerald reputedly keeps those who wear it safely guarded against deception. Some even claim that this deep-green stone acts as a natural lie detector, changing its color whenever someone tells a lie in its presence. Beware if an emerald should happen to fall from its setting, for this is taken as a sign of very bad luck.

Garnet

It has been said that an oath sworn over a garnet can never be broken, and this belief has persisted for many centuries. The garnet has long been regarded as a stone of protection, and was widely used in the Middle Ages to keep demons and night phantoms at bay. Another way in which the garnet is said to protect is by turning a dull color at the moment it "senses" the presence of danger.

Jade

It was once a common belief throughout the country of China that a piece of green jade, when thrown into water, could produce fog or draw down rain or snow from the heavens above. Another ancient Chinese belief concerning jade is that the stone grants prosperity, wisdom, and longevity to those who wear it. Many people in China continue to regard the jade as a sacred stone.

Jet

Long ago, the superstitious believed that when a person wore jet for long periods of time, this black, glass-like stone absorbed part of his or her soul. The ancient Greeks are said to have adorned themselves with jet in order to obtain favor from the goddess Cybele, to whom the jet is sacred.

Lava Rock

It is said that lava rocks are the property of the Hawaiian volcano goddess, Pele, and that bad luck befalls all persons who take them home as souvenirs from the Hawaiian Islands. However, some Hawaiians believe that by presenting Pele with an offering of some sort (such as flowers or fruit) and asking her permission before claiming one of her rocks, a person can avert misfortune. But should bad luck strike after taking possession of a lava rock, the only way to break the jinx is to return the rock to the place from which it was taken and ask for Pele's forgiveness.

Malachite

Gemstone lore holds that malachite warns its wearer of impending peril by shattering into pieces at the approach of danger. This stone of deep green color is also said to protect those who wear it against injuries caused by falling.

Moonstone

Ruled by the moon, the white and lustrous moonstone is said to change color with each lunar phase. Many practitioners of gemstone sorcery also believe that the magickal powers of the moonstone are greatest when the moon is waxing, and diminished when it is on the wane.

Onyx

Within every onyx is imprisoned an evil nocturnal demon that causes terror and nightmares to plague any unfortunate individual who wears this stone to bed or sleeps within its range of influence, according to ancient gemstone legend. Pregnant women were once cautioned to avoid wearing any type of jewelry containing onyx, as the stone was believed to bring on premature labor. Ironically, the same stone is said to aid childbirth when worn by, or placed near, a woman in labor.

Opal

It is thought to be bad luck to wear an engagement ring in which an opal is set, and many superstitious people believe that a woman who does so will be cursed with sorrow and widowhood. Some folks believe that white opals bring bad luck, but black opals are very lucky. And others believe that opals—whether white or black—work as good luck charms only when worn by persons born in October and/or under the astrological sign of Libra. For all other individuals this stone is a bringer of misfortune. According to an ancient Arabian legend, opals fell from the sky in flashes of lightning, acquiring their marvelous colors in the process. The old belief that an opal loses its luster when its owner dies (especially of the plague) dates back to the 14th century, during the time of the widespread epidemic known as the Black Death.

Pearl

There is an old saying that "pearls bring tears," and dreaming about them is an omen of ill luck for the dreamer. It is also supposed to be unlucky to wear pearls at a marriage ceremony or give them to the bride as a wedding present, as they are said to signify tears. Pearls bring good luck only to persons whose birthdays are in the month of June and should never be worn by persons born at any other time of the year. In parts of Great Britain, some people still subscribe to the old superstition that a pearl placed beneath the pillow will help a woman conceive a child. The ancient Egyptians are said to have worn pearls to obtain the favor of Isis (a goddess to whom all pearls are said to be sacred). According to old Christian gem lore, protected by the archangel Gabriel are those who wear or carry a pearl. Chinese folklore holds that pearls fell to earth like raindrops when dragons battled each other among the clouds. Some people even thought pearls to be raindrops swallowed by oysters.

> *"Pearls are intimately connected with the Moon, so much so that some will wear or use them in magic only at night, during the Moon's domain. Because of this connection with lunar energy, they are usually worn by women and rarely by men."*

—Scott Cunningham, *Cunningham's Encyclopedia of Crystal, Gem and Metal Magic*

Quartz Crystal

In ancient times, long before the science of geology was founded, it was commonly believed that quartz crystals were composed of water or pieces of ice that had solidified. An old Japanese legend holds that large quartz crystals were formed from the saliva of the violet dragon, and smaller ones were the congealed breath of the white dragon. In Australia, New Guinea, and other parts of the Pacific, quartz crystals continue to be linked with water and employed by many Shamans in rainmaking ceremonies. Legend has it that the inhabitants of the continent of Atlantis were a highly advanced race that knew how to harness the energy of giant quartz crystals. However, their misuse of the power generated by these stones ultimately triggered cataclysmic Earth changes that destroyed their civilization and caused Atlantis to sink to the bottom of the sea.

> *"Quartz crystal is used as a power amplifier during magic. It is worn or placed on the altar for this purpose."*
>
> —Scott Cunningham

> *"Crystals act like radio transmitters. They have the power to transmit and amplify our energies, good or bad."*
>
> —Joy Gardner, author of *Color and Crystals: A Journey Through the Chakras*

Ruby

According to legend, the color of a ruby darkens to warn its wearer of impending danger. It is said that a ruby will also change color or grow dull when its owner is stricken with illness or succumbs to death. Long ago it was believed that there existed certain rubies that, when submerged in a vessel of water, could increase the temperature of the water and even bring it to the boiling point! The ancients probably saw the fiery red color of the ruby as an indication that this stone possessed the power to generate heat.

Staurolite

Known by the nicknames "fairy cross" or "fairy stone," the staurolite is said to have been formed by the tears of fairies. According to folklore, when the fairies learned of Jesus Christ's crucifixion, they wept tears of sorrow that fell upon the earth and crystallized into staurolites.

Topaz

Centuries ago it was thought by some that wearing a topaz could prevent, as well as cure, insanity. This stone was also credited with having the power to relieve rheumatism and arthritis, prevent sleepwalking, enable invisibility, and guard against sorcery.

Turquoise

The turquoise is generally viewed as a lucky stone, and one that offers its wearer protection against sorcery, poisoning, and accidents (particularly falls from horseback). Native American medicine men have long valued the turquoise for its supposed power to bring forth rain when cast into a river. And when attached to bows, the turquoise is said to prevent arrows from missing their targets. Refrain from wearing a turquoise stone if its color turns to green, lest misfortune befall you in great abundance.

> *"As a compassionate Turquoise that doth tell,*
> *By looking pale the wearer is not well."*

—John Donne (1572–1631), metaphysical poet

Gemstones and Their Pagan Folk Names

Amber: *Good Luck Stone.*

Ammonite: *Serpent Stone.*

Beryl: *Mystic's Stone.*

Chalcedony (rose): *Goddess Stone.*

Danburite: *Shaman's Stone.*

Flint: *Elf-arrow, Elf-shot, Fairy-shot, Hag Stone, Witch Riding Stone.*

Horn Coral: *Dragon Tooth.*

Jade: *Dragon Stone, Dream Stone.*

Jadeite (black): *Devil's Stone.*
Jet: *Witches' Amber.*
Labradorite: *Wizard's Stone.*
Mangano Calcite: *Spirit Stone.*
Moonstone: *Goddess Stone.*
Obsidian: *Stone of Saturn.*
Obsidian (black): *Wizard Stone.*
Onyx: *Demon Stone.*
Quartz Crystal: *Witch's Mirror.*
Septarian Sphere: *Dragon Stone.*
Staurolite: *Fairy Cross, Fairy Tears.*
Turquoise: *Venus Stone.*

Stones and the Spirit World

The association between stones and the spirit world is one that predates recorded history. It was widely believed among primitive people that spirits, both benevolent and malevolent, dwelled within many of the stones of the Earth and could be called upon by "feeding" the stones with the blood of a sacrificed animal, often while reciting certain incantations over it.

Stones were seen by early man not only as the abode of spirits, but as magickal implements to summon spirits and cause them to depart. Shamans valued stones as a natural link to the world of spirit, while others attributed certain minerals (such as chrysolite and sapphire) with the power to prevent ghosts from haunting or harming the living. The natives of Ceylon are said to have used chrysoberyl to keep malevolent spirits at bay. And in medieval times, the burning of powdered jet to drive away evil supernatural entities was a common practice in many parts of Europe, as was the wearing or carrying of stones (particularly amber, coral, and green jasper) as amulets to ward them off.

The quartz crystal has been utilized for centuries as a device for contacting and communicating with the spirit world, and it is not uncommon for many spiritualist mediums to wear crystals in one form or another to facilitate channeling, help establish contact with spirit guides, and protect themselves against any less-than-benevolent spiritual entities that may manifest or "come through" during a séance or channeling session.

Some types of quartz crystals are known as ghost crystals, phantom crystals, specter crystals, and shade crystals. Such names clearly reflect this mineral's otherworldly ties.

Lithoboly—the mysterious hailing of stones by invisible forces—is a phenomenon thought by some to be caused by spirits or, according to folklore, Witches or demons (the latter of which are known as lithobolia). It is frequently connected to places where hauntings or poltergeist activity takes place, and can occur day or night, during any type of weather condition, and either indoors or outside. Some victims or witnesses of lithoboly have reported seeing stones materialize out of thin air inside a room, while others have told stories of being pelted or bombarded by stones that suddenly rained down upon them from the heavens above.

One of the most famous incidents of lithoboly in the United States took place in New Hampshire in the late 17th century. For a period of several months, a wealthy landowner named George Walton, his house, his family, his servants, and even his houseguests, were made the daily targets of an unseen "stone-throwing devil." The phenomena is said to have begun after a land dispute between Walton and one of his neighbors—an elderly woman whom some suspected of practicing the black arts.

In more recent times, paranormal investigators searching for a scientific explanation for ghosts and hauntings have suggested that some stones used for the foundations or walls of buildings are capable of "recording" sounds (such as voices or music), intense human emotions, and even moving or still images. Such stones, under the right circumstances, can also "play back" these captured sights and sounds many years, and even centuries, later.

Such a theory is quite interesting. However, it is not as far-fetched as some might think when considering the fact that many stones contain silica and ferric salts—similar substances to those used in the making of recording tapes. It may also explain why many castles, dungeons, penitentiaries, old hospitals, crypts, and other places constructed with stones, are host to frequent ghost sightings and other paranormal happenings.

In the community of Alton, Illinois (which is said to be the most haunted small city in the United States), there appear to be no shortages of houses exhibiting the classic symptoms of a haunting. Within and around these old and historic dwellings, cold spots, unexplained noises, ghostly manifestations, and disembodied voices have been, and continue to be, reported by witnesses and made the subject of numerous writings and television documentaries.

Interestingly, the foundations and walls of Alton's haunted real estate were constructed with stones from a demolished penitentiary and Confederate Civil War prison where many prisoners and guards had died from an outbreak of smallpox. Some people believe that their human suffering was impressed on the stones of the prison's walls, resulting in what researchers term a "residual haunting."

Back in the 1980s, a team of paranormal investigators studying electronic voice phenomena (E.V.P.) conducted an unusual experiment in an old building with a reputation for being haunted. With a tape recorder running, they fed 20,000 volts of electricity through electrodes attached to one of the building's stone walls. When they later played back the tape to find out what anomalous sounds, if any, had been picked up, they heard strange voices, the sound of music, and even the ticking of a clock. However, no one had been talking, no music had been played, and no ticking clock had been in the area at the time when the recording was made.

The investigators concluded that the silica in the stone walls somehow made a recording of human voices and other sounds that were made in the past, and when the electrons in the silica were triggered, these recordings were played back as ghostly sounds.

Gemstones and the Devil

For protection against assaults by the devil, wear or carry an amulet made of coral or ruby. To make yourself immune to the devil's will, wear a diamond.

The wearing of aquamarine was once believed to give a person great power over the devil. According to a legend from the Middle Ages, if a man hides a piece of aquamarine inside his mouth, he may summon the devil and force him to give a truthful answer to any question that is put before him. It is said that as long as the man keeps the stone in his mouth, the devil can neither harm nor deceive him.

Australian aborigine folklore holds that the opal (a stone considered by many to be the bringer of ill luck) is actually a devil waiting to lure men to their destruction.

A black diamond or any black square-shaped stone, when passed through the smoke of burning elder wood, is supposed to conjure up the devil. Should the evil one refuse to depart, toss some powdered jet into a censer filled with glowing charcoal blocks and, as the smoke rises, command him to be gone. (The burning of jet is also said to be effective for exorcising ghosts and evil spirits and driving away demons.)

The Mystery of the Crystal Skulls

Macabre, mysterious, hypnotic, and even strangely beautiful, crystal skulls are believed by many people to possess extraordinary powers. These objects are frequently used as good luck charms, and some diviners even use them as speculums for scrying.

When handling crystal skulls, some persons (especially psychic-sensitive individuals) report feeling intense energy vibrations emanating from them. Some have fallen into trances and received strange visions (often involving mythical creatures) and others have experienced a heightened sense of psychic awareness and even physical healing.

It is said that crystal skulls store energy like quintessential batteries and are able to record and pictorially replay all events that occur around them. They can also create psychic links between themselves and human beings (and other living things) that come into contact with them. Some people also believe that crystal skulls can speak and hold the power to telepathically communicate with other crystal skulls.

Crystal skulls have gained popularity in recent times, especially among occult practitioners and individuals who practice New Age spirituality. However, the carving of crystals (and other minerals) into the shape of a human skull is a practice that dates back to primitive times. Ancient (pre-Columbian) skulls of clear quartz, amethyst, rose quartz, and smoky quartz have been found in many parts of the world, including Mexico, South America, Russia, Africa, the British Isles, and continental Europe.

While it is known that crystal skulls were crafted by the ancient Egyptians, Aztecs, Mayans, Tibetans, and Native American Indians at approximately the same time in human evolution, their true religious and/or magickal significance remains one of the great mysteries of the world.

Some authors on the subject have theorized that crystal skulls were created by ancient civilizations for use in sacrificial rites and/or to symbolize their god or goddess of death. Others believe that they were used as tools for divining, healing, warding off evil spirits and/or attracting the protection of beneficent ones.

An ancient Native American legend claims that the Great Spirit created 13 crystal skulls, which he encoded with information disclosing the true purpose and future destiny of mankind. The legend also says that when the human race is sufficiently developed, these 13 crystal skulls will be discovered and the secrets they hold will be revealed.

According to some New Age gurus, the priests of Atlantis possessed 12 crystal skulls, which, when placed in groups of three on a circular astrological altar of copper, bronze, silver, and gold, would cause an etheric 13th skull to manifest in the center of the ring. The 13th skull completed the circuit and gave the ring of crystal skulls the power to transmit and receive data between "Star Beings" and the human race.

The most famous of all ancient crystal skulls is one that was allegedly discovered in 1927 by F. A. Mitchell-Hedges atop the ruins of an ancient Mayan temple in British Honduras, now Belize. (Documents in the British Museum reveal that the artifact was actually purchased by Mitchell-Hedges at a Sotheby's auction in London in 1943.) Fashioned from a solitary block of clear quartz, it measures 5 inches in height, with a length of 7 inches and a width of 5 inches—approximately the size of a small human cranium. It is the only known crystal skull possessing a removable jaw.

Tests conducted in 1970 at California's Hewlett-Packard Laboratories (a leading facility for crystal research) revealed that no metal tools of any kind had been used in the making of the nearly flawless Mitchell-Hedges skull. Art restorer Frank Dorland, who had researched the skull for a six-year period from 1964 to 1970 and oversaw the testing, concluded that the crystal had likely been chiseled into a rough form with a diamond, and its finer shaping, grinding, and polishing carried out by countless applications of a silicon sand and water solution—a process that would have required more than three centuries of nonstop labor!

Dorland, who authored a book called *Holy Ice: Bridge to the Subconscious*, wrote that when he meditated with the crystal skull, he would "inwardly see the face of a young woman." He believed that the skull stimulated "an unknown part of the brain, opening a psychic door to the absolute," and also claimed that it spontaneously produced holographic images and emitted strange sounds that coincided with certain planetary configurations.

Another famous crystal skull of ancient origin is the so-called Museum of Mankind Skull, which is currently owned by the British Museum and on display at the Museum of Mankind in London. Believed to have been made by the Aztecs, this skull is said to possess strange hypnotic powers and must be covered at night with a black cloth to prevent those who work in the museum after hours from gazing at it and falling into a trance.

> *"I personally feel that the Crystal Skulls are not only here to share ancient knowledge and wisdom, but to assist in awakening our race to higher spiritual laws and understanding of itself."*
>
> —Joshua Shapiro, coauthor of *Mysteries of the Crystal Skulls Revealed*

Appendix A

A Calendar of Daily Stones

The charts on the following pages contain gemstones that correspond to each day of the year. Wear a stone on its designated date to enjoy the magickal properties that it possesses.

[Based on information from *Llewellyn's 1995 Magical Almanac*, edited by Cynthia Ahlquist.]

	January	February	March	April
1	Citrine	Rhodochrosite	Rhodochrosite	Blue Lace Agate
2	Selenite	Tourmaline	Turquoise	Carnelian
3	Onxy	Abalone	Unikite	White Coral
4	Citrine	Azurite	Obsidian	Bloodstone
5	Peridot	Fire Agate	Fire Agate	Citrine
6	Rose Quartz	Crystals	Milky Quartz	Aventurine
7	Lapis Lazuli	Jet or Black Coral	Hematite	Mother of Pearl
8	Tiger's Eye	Light Carnelian	Tiger's Eye	Hematite
9	Mother of Pearl	Chrysocolla	Aventurine	Fire Agate
10	Ruby	Rhodochrosite	Abalone	Fluorite
11	Moonstone	Smokey Quartz	Sodalite	Carnelian
12	Malachite	Tiger's Eye	Rutilated Quartz	Light Carnelian
13	Unikite	Pale Amethyst	Silver	Amethyst
14	Hematite	Obsidian	Onxy	Moonstone
15	Amber	Moonstone	Light Carnelian	Smokey Quartz
16	Hematite	Aventurine	Chrysocolla	Rutilated Quartz
17	Obsidian	Rose Quartz	Pink Tourmaline	Selenite
18	Tiger's Eye	Lapis Lazuli	Obsidian	Obsidian
19	Turquoise	Carnelian	Opal	Yellow Jasper
20	Abalone	Abalone	Hematite	Emerald
21	Azurite	Bloodstone	Garnet	Opal
22	Azurite	Amber	Yellow Jasper	Hematite
23	Carnelian	Amethyst	Malachite	Opal
24	Milky Quartz	Opal	Moonstone	Pearl
25	Red Jasper	Blue Coral	Quartz Crystal	Hematite
26	Yellow Jasper	Opal	Citrine	Moonstone
27	Amethyst	Flourite	Abalone	Toumaline
28	Opal	Apache Tears	Cinnabar	Rainbow Quartz
29	Fire Agate	(Diamond)	Citrine	Sodalite
30	Marble	———	Amazonite	Rhodochrosite
31	Cinnabar	———	Rose Quartz	———

	May	June	July	August
1	Turquoise	Green Quartz	Smokey Quartz	Red Amber
2	Jet or Black Coral	Moonstone	Carnelian	Yellow Jasper
3	Rhodochrosite	Sapphire	Milky Quartz	Green Quartz
4	Aquamarine	Carnelian	Carnelian	Rhodochrosite
5	Abalone	Selenite	Citrine	Crystals
6	Blue Tiger's Eye	Cinnabar	Aventurine	Carnelian
7	Amber	Yellow Fluorite	Rainbow Quartz	Milky Quartz
8	Marble	Chrysocolla	Obsidian	Granite
9	Apache Tears	Unikite	Amber	Moonstone
10	Citrine	Petrified Wood	Amethyst	Malachite
11	Malachite	Rutilated Quartz	Onyx	Abalone
12	Pink Tourmaline	White Coral	Rhodochrosite	Sodalite
13	Lapis Lazuli	Red Jasper	Peridot	Amber
14	Rhodochrosite	Citrine	Moonstone	Moonstone
15	Abalone	Bloodstone	Sodalite	Coral
16	Red Amber	Peach Carnelian	Rhodochrosite	Citrine
17	Light Carnelian	Hematite	Selenite	Emerald
18	Jade	Opal	Garnet	Rose Quartz
19	Moonstone	Pale Amethyst	Light Carnelian	Obsidian
20	Sodalite	Coral	Bloodstone	Fire Agate
21	Fire Agate	Light Carnelian	Rhodochrosite	White Coral
22	White Agate	Malachite	Lapis Lazuli	Ruby
23	Granite	Abalone	Fire Agate	Rhodochrosite
24	Yellow Fluorite	Obsidian	Crystals	Chrysocolla
25	Amazonite	Fire Agate	Cinnabar	Opal
26	Mother of Pearl	Moonstone	Yellow Jasper	Blue Tiger's Eye
27	Azurite	Marble	Green Fluorite	Opal
28	Opal	Amber	Opal	Hematite
29	Shells	Emerald	Hematite	Apache Tears
30	Ruby	Rainbow Quartz	Citrine	Tiger's Eye
31	Tiger's Eye	———	Abalone	Amazonite

	September	October	November	December
1	Pink Tourmaline	Rhodochrosite	Amber	Unikite
2	Fluorite	Mother of Pearl	Jade	Petrified Wood
3	Carnelian	Coral	Moonstone	Fire Agate
4	Mother of Pearl	Tiger's Eye	Sapphire	Crystals
5	Garnet	Aventurine	Carnelian	Cinnabar
6	Amber	Moonstone	Turquoise	Citrine
7	Green Fluorite	Sodalite	Cinnabar	Emerald
8	Unikite	Citrine	Citrine	Mother of Pearl
9	Petrified Wood	Rainbow Quartz	Amazonite	Smokey Quartz
10	Citrine	Obsidian	Pink Tourmaline	Amber
11	Hematite	Rhodochrosite	Fluorite	Hematite
12	Red Jasper	Jade	Rhodochrosite	Onyx
13	Rhodochrosite	Pink Tourmaline	Selenite	Light Carnelian
14	Malachite	Blue Coral	Obsidian Yellow	Peridot
15	Abalone	Amber	Fluorite	Rainbow Quartz
16	Blue Coral	Marble	Amethyst	Hematite
17	Rhodochrosite	Red Jasper	Opal	Rhodochrosite
18	Pale Amethyst	Yellow Jasper	Black Lace Agate	White Agate
19	Fire Agate	Green Fluorite	Tiger's Eye	Carnelian
20	Light Carnelian	Opal	Pearl	Moonstone
21	Tourmaline	Smokey Quartz	Red Amber	Tourmaline
22	Peach Carnelian	Gold	Tiger's Eye	Abalone
23	Lapis Lazuli	Fluorite	Malachite	Sodalite
24	Fire Agate	Ruby	Rainbow Quartz	Opal
25	Selenite	Light Carnelian	Hematite	Crystals
26	Coral	Bloodstone	Carnelian	Red Amber
27	Citrine	Rose Quartz	Marble	Citrine
28	Amethyst	Blue Tiger's Eye	Coral	Emerald
29	Opal	Rutilated Quartz	Rhodochrosite	Unikite
30	Obsidian	Pale Amethyst	Green Quartz	Lapis Lazuli
31	———	Onyx	———	Amber

Appendix B

Correspondences

The following is an alphabetical list of gemstones and their correspondences with the Elements, energy types, numerical vibrations, planets, and Zodiac signs.

Acanthite
Elemental ruler: Earth
Energy: receptive
Numerical vibration: 9
Planetary ruler: Saturn
Zodiac sign: Scorpio

Actinolite
Elemental ruler: Earth
Energy: receptive
Numerical vibration: 9
Planetary ruler: Venus
Zodiac sign: Scorpio

Adamite
Elemental ruler: Earth
Energy: projective/receptive
Numerical vibration: 8
Planetary ruler: Venus
Zodiac sign: Cancer

Agate (Angel Wing)
Elemental ruler: unknown
Energy: receptive
Numerical vibration: 9
Planetary ruler: Mercury
Zodiac signs: Aries and Taurus

Agate (Blood)
Elemental ruler: Fire
Energy: projective
Numerical vibration: 1
Planetary ruler: Mercury
Zodiac sign: Aquarius

Agate (Blue Lace)
Elemental ruler: Water
Energy: receptive
Numerical vibration: 5
Planetary ruler: Mercury
Zodiac sign: Pisces

Agate (Botswana)
Elemental ruler: unknown
Energy: receptive
Numerical vibration: 3
Planetary ruler: Jupiter
Zodiac sign: Scorpio

Agate (Brasilian)
Elemental ruler: various
Energy: projective/receptive
Numerical vibration: 2
Planetary ruler: Mercury
Zodiac sign: Aries

Agate (Dendritic)
Elemental ruler: Air
Energy: receptive
Numerical vibration: 3
Planetary ruler: Mercury
Zodiac sign: Gemini

Agate (Fire)
Elemental ruler: Fire
Energy: projective
Numerical vibration: 9
Planetary ruler: Mercury
Zodiac sign: Aries

Agate (Green)
Elemental ruler: Earth
Energy: receptive
Numerical vibration: 2
Planetary ruler: Mercury
Zodiac sign: unknown

Agate (Moss)
Elemental ruler: Earth
Energy: receptive
Numerical vibration: 1
Planetary ruler: Mercury
Zodiac sign: Virgo

Agate (Purple Sage)
Elemental ruler: unknown
Energy: receptive
Numerical vibration: 1
Planetary ruler: Mercury
Zodiac signs: Scorpio and Virgo

Agate (Regency Rose)
Elemental ruler: Water
Energy: receptive
Numerical vibration: 6
Planetary ruler: Mercury
Zodiac sign: Virgo

Agate (Rose-Eye)

Elemental ruler: Water
Energy: receptive
Numerical vibration: 9
Planetary rulers: Mercury and Venus
Zodiac sign: Gemini

Agate (Snakeskin)

Elemental ruler: unknown
Energy: receptive
Numerical vibration: 2
Planetary ruler: Mercury
Zodiac sign: Scorpio

Alabaster

Elemental ruler: Water
Energy: receptive
Numerical vibration: 7
Planetary ruler: Moon
Zodiac sign: Sagittarius

Albite

Elemental ruler: unknown
Energy: receptive
Numerical vibration: 4
Planetary ruler: unknown
Zodiac sign: Aquarius

Alexandrite

Elemental ruler: Earth
Energy: receptive
Numerical vibration: 5
Planetary ruler: Venus
Zodiac sign: Scorpio

Almandine

Elemental ruler: Water
Energy: receptive/projective
Numerical vibration: 1
Planetary ruler: unknown
Zodiac signs: Scorpio and Virgo

Alurgite

Elemental ruler: Fire
Energy: projective
Numerical vibration: 3
Planetary ruler: Mars
Zodiac sign: Leo

Amazonite

Elemental ruler: Earth
Energy: receptive
Numerical vibration: 5
Planetary ruler: Uranus
Zodiac sign: Virgo

Amber

Elemental ruler: Fire
Energy: projective
Numerical vibration: 3
Planetary ruler: Sun
Zodiac signs: Leo and Aquarius

Amblygonite

Elemental ruler: Water
Energy: receptive
Numerical vibration: 6
Planetary ruler: unknown
Zodiac sign: Taurus

Amethyst

Elemental ruler: Water

Energy: receptive

Numerical vibration: 3

Planetary rulers: Jupiter and Neptune

Zodiac signs: Aquarius, Capricorn, Pisces, and Virgo

Ametrine

Elemental rulers: Water and Fire

Energy: projective/receptive

Numerical vibration: 4

Planetary rulers: Jupiter and the Sun

Zodiac sign: Libra

Andalusite

Elemental ruler: various

Energy: projective/receptive

Numerical vibration: 7

Planetary ruler: various

Zodiac sign: Virgo

Angelite

Elemental ruler: Water

Energy: receptive

Numerical vibration: 1

Planetary rulers: The Moon and Neptune

Zodiac sign: Aquarius

Apache Gold

Elemental ruler: Fire

Energy: projective/receptive

Numerical vibration: 9

Planetary ruler: Sun

Zodiac sign: Leo

Apache Tear

Elemental ruler: Fire

Energy: projective

Numerical vibration: 6

Planetary ruler: Saturn

Zodiac sign: Aries

Aquamarine

Elemental ruler: Water

Energy: receptive

Numerical vibration: 1

Planetary ruler: Moon

Zodiac signs: Aries, Gemini, and Pisces

Aventurine

Elemental ruler: Air

Energy: projective

Numerical vibration: 3

Planetary ruler: Mercury

Zodiac sign: Aries

Azurite

Elemental ruler: Water

Energy: receptive

Numerical vibration: 1

Planetary ruler: Venus

Zodiac sign: Sagittarius

Basinite

Elemental ruler: Earth
Energy: receptive
Numerical vibration: 7
Planetary ruler: Saturn
Zodiac sign: Sagittarius

Beaverite

Elemental ruler: Fire
Energy: projective
Numerical vibration: 6
Planetary ruler: Mercury
Zodiac sign: Libra

Beryl

Elemental ruler: Water
Energy: receptive
Numerical vibration: 8
Planetary ruler: Mars
Zodiac sign: Scorpio

Beryl (Golden)

Elemental ruler: Fire
Energy: projective
Numerical vibration: 1
Planetary ruler: Sun
Zodiac sign: Leo

Bloodstone (also known as Heliotrope)

Elemental ruler: Fire
Energy: projective
Numerical vibration: 4
Planetary ruler: Mars
Zodiac signs: Aries, Libra, Pisces

Brazilianite

Elemental ruler: Fire
Energy: projective
Numerical vibration: 9
Planetary ruler: Mercury
Zodiac sign: Capricorn

Calcite

Elemental ruler: Water
Energy: receptive
Numerical vibration: 8
Planetary ruler: Moon
Zodiac sign: Cancer

Calcite (Blue)

Elemental ruler: Water
Energy: receptive
Numerical vibration: 3
Planetary ruler: Venus
Zodiac sign: unknown

Calcite (Green)

Elemental ruler: Earth
Energy: receptive
Numerical vibration: 3
Planetary ruler: Venus
Zodiac sign: unknown

Calcite (Orange)

Elemental ruler: Fire
Energy: projective
Numerical vibration: 5
Planetary ruler: Sun
Zodiac sign: unknown

Calcite (Pink)
Elemental ruler: Water
Energy: receptive
Numerical vibration: 4
Planetary ruler: Venus
Zodiac sign: unknown

Caledonite
Elemental ruler: Water
Energy: receptive
Numerical vibration: 7
Planetary ruler: Neptune
Zodiac sign: Pisces

Carnelian
Elemental ruler: Fire
Energy: projective
Numerical vibration: 5
Planetary ruler: Sun
Zodiac signs: Cancer, Leo, and Taurus

Catlinite (also known as Pipestone)
Elemental ruler: Fire
Energy: projective
Numerical vibration: 3
Planetary rulers: Sun and Mars
Zodiac sign: Sagittarius

Cat's Eye
Elemental ruler: Earth
Energy: projective
Numerical vibration: 6

Planetary ruler: Venus
Zodiac signs: Aries, Capricorn, and Taurus

Celestite
Elemental ruler: Water
Energy: receptive
Numerical vibration: 8
Planetary rulers: Venus and Neptune
Zodiac sign: Gemini

Ceruleite
Elemental ruler: Water
Energy: receptive
Numerical vibration: 8
Planetary ruler: Neptune
Zodiac sign: Taurus

Chalcedony
Elemental ruler: Water
Energy: receptive
Numerical vibration: 9
Planetary ruler: Moon
Zodiac signs: Cancer and Sagittarius

Chrysoberyl (Yellow or Honey)
Elemental ruler: Air
Energy: projective
Numerical vibration: 6
Planetary ruler: Sun
Zodiac sign: Leo

Chrysocolla
Elemental ruler: Water
Energy: receptive
Numerical vibration: 5
Planetary ruler: Venus
Zodiac signs: Gemini, Taurus, and Virgo

Chrysoprase
Elemental ruler: Earth
Energy: receptive
Numerical vibration: 3
Planetary ruler: Venus
Zodiac sign: Libra

Cinnabar
Elemental ruler: Fire
Energy: projective
Numerical vibration: 8
Planetary ruler: Mars
Zodiac sign: Leo

Citrine
Elemental ruler: Fire
Energy: projective
Numerical vibration: 6
Planetary ruler: Sun
Zodiac signs: Aries, Gemini, Leo, and Libra

Coal
Elemental ruler: Earth
Energy: receptive
Numerical vibration: 4
Planetary ruler: Saturn
Zodiac sign: Capricorn

Colemanite
Elemental ruler: Water
Energy: receptive
Numerical vibration: 7
Planetary ruler: Moon
Zodiac sign: Aries

Columbite
Elemental ruler: Earth
Energy: receptive
Numerical vibration: 1
Planetary ruler: Saturn
Zodiac sign: Aquarius

Coral
Elemental ruler: Water
Energy: receptive
Numerical vibration: 4
Planetary ruler: Venus
Zodiac sign: Pisces

Coral (Black)
Elemental rulers: Water and Earth
Energy: receptive
Numerical vibration: 6
Planetary ruler: Saturn
Zodiac signs: Capricorn and Scorpio

Coral (Blue)

Elemental ruler: Water

Energy: receptive

Numerical vibration: 8

Planetary ruler: Neptune

Zodiac signs: Aquarius and Sagittarius

Coral (Red)

Elemental ruler: Fire

Energy: projective

Numerical vibration: 4

Planetary ruler: Mars

Zodiac sign: Libra

Coral (Pink)

Elemental ruler: Water

Energy: receptive

Numerical vibration: 9

Planetary ruler: Venus

Zodiac sign: Cancer

Coral (White)

Elemental ruler: Water

Energy: receptive

Numerical vibration: 6

Planetary ruler: Moon

Zodiac sign: Pisces

Cornetite

Elemental ruler: Earth

Energy: receptive

Numerical vibration: 1

Planetary ruler: Venus

Zodiac sign: Aries

Damsonite

Elemental ruler: Water

Energy: receptive

Numerical vibration: 1

Planetary ruler: Jupiter

Zodiac signs: Libra and Virgo

Diamond

Elemental ruler: Fire

Energy: projective

Numerical vibration: 6

Planetary ruler: Sun

Zodiac signs: Aries, Leo, Taurus

Dolomite

Elemental ruler: unknown

Energy: projective/receptive

Numerical vibration: 3

Planetary ruler: unknown

Zodiac sign: Aries

Dumontite

Elemental ruler: Fire

Energy: projective

Numerical vibration: 4

Planetary ruler: Sun

Zodiac sign: Libra

Emerald

Elemental ruler: Earth

Energy: receptive

Numerical vibration: 4

Planetary ruler: Venus

Zodiac signs: Aries, Gemini, and Taurus

Flint

Elemental ruler: Fire
Energy: projective
Numerical vibration: 7
Planetary ruler: Mars
Zodiac sign: Scorpio

Garnet

Elemental ruler: Fire
Energy: projective
Numerical vibration: 2
Planetary ruler: Mars
Zodiac signs: Aquarius,
  Capricorn, Leo, and Virgo

Heliotrope (also known as Bloodstone)

Elemental ruler: Fire
Energy: projective
Numerical vibration: 4
Planetary ruler: Mars
Zodiac signs: Aries, Libra, and
  Pisces

Hematite

Elemental ruler: Fire
Energy: projective
Numerical vibration: 9
Planetary ruler: Saturn
Zodiac signs: Aquarius and Aries

Hyacinth or Jacinth (Red Zircon)

Elemental ruler: Fire

Energy: projective
Numerical vibration: 7 or 2
Planetary ruler: Sun
Zodiac sign: unknown

Jade

Elemental ruler: Water
Energy: receptive
Numerical vibration: 2
Planetary ruler: Venus
Zodiac signs: Aries, Gemini,
  Libra, and Taurus

Jasper (Brown)

Elemental ruler: Earth
Energy: receptive
Numerical vibration: 6
Planetary ruler: Saturn
Zodiac sign: Sagittarius

Jasper (Green)

Elemental ruler: Earth
Energy: receptive
Numerical vibration: 1
Planetary ruler: Venus
Zodiac sign: Gemini

Jasper (Mottled)

Elemental ruler: Air
Energy: projective
Numerical vibration: 5
Planetary ruler: Mercury
Zodiac sign: Gemini

Jasper (Red)

Elemental ruler: Fire
Energy: projective
Numerical vibration: 6
Planetary ruler: Mars
Zodiac sign: Taurus

Jet

Elemental ruler: Earth
Energy: receptive
Numerical vibration: 8
Planetary ruler: Saturn
Zodiac sign: Capricorn

Kunzite

Elemental ruler: Earth
Energy: receptive
Numerical vibration: 7
Planetary rulers: Venus and
    Pluto
Zodiac signs: Leo, Scorpio,
    and Taurus

Lapis Lazuli

Elemental ruler: Water
Energy: receptive
Numerical vibration: 3
Planetary ruler: Venus
Zodiac sign: Sagittarius

Lava

Elemental ruler: Fire
Energy: projective

Numerical vibration: 9
Planetary ruler: Mars
Zodiac sign: Aries

Lepidolite

Elemental ruler: Water
Energy: receptive
Numerical vibration: 8
Planetary rulers: Jupiter and
    Neptune
Zodiac sign: Libra

Malachite

Elemental ruler: Earth
Energy: receptive
Numerical vibration: 9
Planetary ruler: Venus
Zodiac signs: Capricorn and
    Scorpio

Marble

Elemental ruler: Water
Energy: receptive
Numerical vibration: 6
Planetary ruler: Moon
Zodiac sign: Cancer

Mica

Elemental ruler: Air
Energy: projective
Numerical vibration: 8
Planetary ruler: Mercury
Zodiac sign: Aquarius

Moonstone
Elemental ruler: Water
Energy: receptive
Numerical vibration: 4
Planetary ruler: Moon
Zodiac signs: Cancer, Libra, and
Scorpio

Mother-of-Pearl
Elemental ruler: Water
Energy: receptive
Numerical vibration: 8
Planetary ruler: Moon
Zodiac sign: Cancer and Pisces

Obsidian
Elemental ruler: Fire
Energy: projective
Numerical vibration: 1
Planetary ruler: Saturn
Zodiac sign: Sagittarius

Olivine
Elemental ruler: Earth
Energy: receptive
Numerical vibration: 5
Planetary ruler: Venus
Zodiac sign: Virgo

Onyx
Elemental ruler: Fire
Energy: projective
Numerical vibration: 6
Planetary rulers: Mars and Saturn
Zodiac sign: Leo

Opal
Elemental ruler: Air
Energy: projective/receptive
Numerical vibration: 8
Planetary ruler: Moon
Zodiac sign: Libra

Pearl
Elemental ruler: Water
Energy: receptive
Numerical vibration: 7
Planetary ruler: Moon
Zodiac signs: Cancer and
Gemini

Peridot
Elemental ruler: Earth
Energy: receptive
Numerical vibration: 6
Planetary ruler: Venus
Zodiac signs: Leo, Sagittarius,
Scorpio, and Virgo

Pipestone (also known as Catlinite)
Elemental ruler: Fire
Energy: projective
Numerical vibration: 3
Planetary rulers: Sun and Mars
Zodiac sign: Sagittarius

Pumice

Elemental ruler: Air
Energy: projective
Numerical vibration: 4
Planetary ruler: Mercury
Zodiac sign: Capricorn

Quartz (Quartz Crystal)

Elemental rulers: Water and Fire
Energy: projective/receptive
Numerical vibration: 4
Planetary rulers: Moon and Sun
Zodiac sign: Cancer

Quartz (Rose)

Elemental ruler: Water
Energy: receptive
Numerical vibration: 7
Planetary ruler: Venus
Zodiac signs: Libra and Taurus

Rhodochrosite

Elemental ruler: Fire
Energy: projective
Numerical vibration: 4
Planetary ruler: Mars
Zodiac signs: Leo and Scorpio

Rhodonite

Elemental ruler: Fire
Energy: projective
Numerical vibration: 9
Planetary ruler: Mars
Zodiac sign: Taurus

Ruby

Elemental ruler: Fire
Energy: projective
Numerical vibration: 3
Planetary ruler: Sun
Zodiac signs: Cancer, Leo, Sagittarius, and Scorpio

Sapphire

Elemental ruler: Water
Energy: receptive
Numerical vibration: 2
Planetary ruler: Moon
Zodiac signs: Libra, Sagittarius, and Virgo

Sapphire (Black)

Elemental ruler: Earth
Energy: receptive
Numerical vibration: 4
Planetary ruler: Saturn
Zodiac sign: Sagittarius

Sapphire (Blue)

Elemental ruler: Water
Energy: receptive
Numerical vibration: 6
Planetary ruler: Neptune
Zodiac sign: Gemini

Sapphire (Green)

Elemental ruler: Earth
Energy: receptive
Numerical vibration: 6
Planetary ruler: Venus
Zodiac signs: Gemini and Leo

Sapphire (Indigo)

Elemental ruler: Water
Energy: receptive
Numerical vibration: 6
Planetary ruler: Neptune
Zodiac sign: Sagittarius

Sapphire (Purple)

Elemental ruler: Air
Energy: receptive
Numerical vibration: 9
Planetary ruler: Jupiter
Zodiac sign: Virgo

Sapphire (Star)

Elemental ruler: Water
Energy: receptive
Numerical vibration: 6
Planetary ruler: Jupiter
Zodiac signs: Capricorn and
    Sagittarius

Sapphire (White)

Elemental ruler: Water
Energy: receptive
Numerical vibration: 4
Planetary ruler: Moon
Zodiac sign: Libra

Sapphire (Yellow)

Elemental ruler: Air
Energy: projective
Numerical vibration: 4
Planetary ruler: Sun
Zodiac sign: Leo

Sardonyx

Elemental ruler: Fire
Energy: projective
Numerical vibration: 3
Planetary rulers: Mars and
    Mercury
Zodiac signs: Aries and Virgo

Selenite

Elemental ruler: Water
Energy: receptive
Numerical vibration: 8
Planetary ruler: Moon
Zodiac signs: Cancer and Taurus

Serpentine

Elemental ruler: Fire
Energy: projective
Numerical vibration: 8
Planetary ruler: Saturn
Zodiac sign: Gemini

Sodalite

Elemental ruler: Water
Energy: receptive
Numerical vibration: 4
Planetary ruler: Venus
Zodiac sign: Sagittarius

Sphene

Elemental ruler: Air
Energy: projective
Numerical vibration: 4
Planetary ruler: Mercury
Zodiac sign: Sagittarius

Spinel
Elemental ruler: Fire
Energy: projective
Numerical vibration: 3
Planetary ruler: Pluto
Zodiac signs: Aries and
　Sagittarius

Staurolite
Elemental rulers: all Elements
Energy: projective/receptive
Numerical vibration: 5
Planetary ruler: unknown
Zodiac sign: Pisces

Sugilite
Elemental ruler: Water
Energy: receptive
Numerical vibration: 3
Planetary ruler: Jupiter
Zodiac sign: Virgo

Sunstone
Elemental ruler: Fire
Energy: projective
Numerical vibration: 1
Planetary ruler: Sun
Zodiac signs: Leo and Libra

Tiger's Eye
Elemental ruler: Fire
Energy: projective
Numerical vibration: 4
Planetary ruler: Sun
Zodiac sign: Capricorn

Topaz
Elemental ruler: Fire
Energy: projective
Numerical vibration: 6
Planetary ruler: Sun
Zodiac sign: Sagittarius

Tourmaline (Black)
Elemental ruler: Earth
Energy: receptive
Numerical vibrations: 3 and 4
Planetary ruler: Saturn
Zodiac sign: Capricorn

Tourmaline (Blue)
Elemental ruler: Water
Energy: receptive
Numerical vibration: 6
Planetary ruler: Venus
Zodiac signs: Libra and Taurus

Tourmaline (Green)
Elemental ruler: Earth
Energy: receptive
Numerical vibration: 6
Planetary ruler: Venus
Zodiac sign: Capricorn

Tourmaline (Pink)
Elemental ruler: Water
Energy: receptive
Numerical vibration: 7
Planetary ruler: Venus
Zodiac sign: Libra

Tourmaline (Rubellite)

Elemental ruler: Fire

Energy: projective

Numerical vibration: 5

Planetary ruler: Mars

Zodiac signs: Scorpio and
Sagittarius

Tourmaline (Watermelon)

Elemental rulers: Fire and Water

Energy: projective/receptive

Numerical vibration: 2

Planetary rulers: Venus and
Mars

Zodiac signs: Gemini and Virgo

Turquoise

Elemental ruler: Earth

Energy: receptive

Numerical vibration: 1

Planetary rulers: Venus and
Neptune

Zodiac signs: Pisces, Sagittarius,
and Scorpio

Zircon

Elemental ruler: Fire

Energy: projective

Numerical vibration: 4

Planetary ruler: Sun

Zodiac signs: Leo, Sagittarius,
and Virgo

Appendix C
Pagan Gods and Their Sacred Gemstones

Pagan God	Pantheon	Sacred Gemstone(s)
Aesculapius	Roman	Agate
Apollo	Greek	Amber and Sapphire
Bacchus	Roman	Amethyst
Beel-Zebul (Lord of Zebulon)	Semetic	Green Beryl
Buddha	Buddhist/Indian	Jade and Turquoise
Chalchiutotolin	Aztec	Jade
Cupid	Roman	Opal
Damballah	African	Serpentine
Daramulun	Australian	Quartz Crystal
Dionysus	Greek	Amethyst
Ganesha	Hindu/Indian	Ivory
Great Rainbow Snake	Australian	Mother of Pearl, Quartz Crystal, and Serpentine
Great Spirit	Native American	Turquoise
Helios	Greek	Heliodor (Golden Beryl)
Hercules	Roman	Beryl and Opal
Itzcoliuhqui	Aztec	Obsidian
Ixquuimilli-Itzlacoliuhqui	Aztec	Obsidian

(cont'd)

Pagan God	Pantheon	Sacred Gemstone(s)
Jupiter	Roman	Topaz
Klehanoai	Navajo	Quartz Crystal
Mara	Hindu	Aquamarine and Beryl
Mars	Roman	Onyx and Sardonyx
Mercury (Mercurius)	Roman	Emerald
Neptune (Neptunus)	Roman	Beryl and Pearl
Olokun	African	Coral and Quartz Crystal
Orunmila	African	Ivory
Pan	Greek	Jet
Poseidon	Greek	Beryl and Pearl
Ra	Egyptian	Tiger's Eye and Topaz
Sin	Babylonian	Lapis Lazuli
Sopedu	Egyptian	Turquoise
Tezcatlipoca	Aztec	Black Obsidian
Ti-Tsang Wang	Chinese	Pearl
Vishnu	Hindu/Indian	Emerald

Appendix D
Pagan Goddesses and Their Sacred Gemstones

Pagan Goddess	Pantheon	Sacred Gemstone(s)
Allat	Arabian	White Granite
Amberella	Lithuanian	Amber
Amethyst	Greek	Amethyst
Bast (Bastet)	Egyptian	Cat's Eye
Ceres	Roman	Emerald
Chalchiuhtlicue	Aztec	Jade
Coatlicue	Aztex	Jade
Cybele	Phrygian	Jet
Diana	Roman	Amethyst, Moonstone, and Pearl
Electra	Greek	Amber
Esmeralda	South American	Emerald
Estsanatlehi	Navajo	Turquoise
Freya	Nordic/German	Amber and Pearl
Hathor	Egyptian	Turquoise
Hecate	Greek	Black Stone (Baetylic, a type of meteorite), Moonstone, Pearl, Quartz Crystal, and Star Sapphire
The Heliades (Electrides)	Greek	Amber
Hine-Nui-Te-Po	Polynesian	Jade
Ho Hsien-Ku	Chinese	Mother of Pearl

 (cont'd)

Pagan Goddess	Pantheon	Sacred Gemstone(s)
Isis	Egyptian	Carnelian, Coral, Emerald, Jasper, Lapis Lazuli, Moonstone, and Pearl
Itzpapalotl	Aztec	Obsidian
Itzpapalotl-Itzcueye	Aztec	Obsidian
Jurate	Lithuanian	Amber
Kuan Yin	Chinese	Jade and Pearl
Lakshmi	Hindu/Indian	Pearl
Maat	Egyptian	Jade
Maha-Sarasvati	Buddhist	Pearl
Marian	Middle Eastern	Pearl
Medea	Greek	Coral
Muttlamman (Pearl Mother)	Indian	Pearl
Nuit	Egyptian	Lapis Lazuli
Oshun	African	Amber and Coral
Pele	Polynesian	Lava Rock, Obsidian, Olivine, Peridot, and Pumice
Sekhmet	Egyptian	Tiger's Eye
Selene	Greek	Moonstone and Selenite
Surdurjaya	Buddhist	Emerald
Tiamat	Babylonian	Beryl
Venus	Roman	Amethyst, Coral, Emerald, Lapis Lazuli, Onyx, Pearl, and Pink Quartz
Vesta	Roman	Chrysoprase
Yemaya	African	Coral, Pearl, and Quartz Crystal

Appendix E

Sacred Gemstones of the Tree of Life

The Tree of Life in the Qabalistic tradition contains 10 *sephiroth*, which represent different aspects of the Divine and are each a level of attainment in knowledge. The first *sephirah* (Kether) is believed by Qabalists to have emanated from God, and the fourth (Chesed) through the 10th (Malkuth) are said to correspond to the seven energy centers (charkas) located along the human spine.

Qabalists also believe that, through meditation and contemplation, an individual whose body, mind, and spirit have been purified can ascend the Tree of Life and attain enlightenment.

According to Aleister Crowley, the stones attributed to the 10 sephiroth and the 22 paths of the Tree of Life are as follows:

1. **Kether** (Crown): diamond.
2. **Chokhmah** (Wisdom): star ruby and turquoise.
3. **Binah** (Understanding): star sapphire and pearl.
4. **Chesed** (Mercy): amethyst and sapphire.

5. **Geburah** (Judgment): ruby.

6. **Tipheret** (Beauty): topaz and yellow diamond.

7. **Netzach** (Victory): emerald.

8. **Hod** (Glory): opal, especially fire opal.

9. **Yesod** (Foundation): quartz.

10. **Malkuth** (Kingdom): rock crystal.

11. Topaz or chalcedony.

12. Opal or agate.

13. Moonstone, pearl, or crystal.

14. Emerald or turquoise.

15. Ruby.

16. Topaz.

17. Alexandrite, tourmaline, or Iceland spar.

18. Amber.

19. Cat's eye.

20. Peridot.

21. Amethyst or lapis lazuli.

22. Emerald.

23. Beryl or aquamarine.

24. Snakestone.

25. Jacinth.

26. Black diamond.

27. Ruby, or any red stone.

28. Artificial glass.

29. Pearl.

30. Chrysoleth.

31. Fire Opal.

32. Onyx.

Appendix F

Gemstones of the Eight Witches' Sabbats

any Witches, solitaries as well as those who work their magick in covens or circles, observe eight annual solar festivals or Sabbats (known collectively as the "Wheel of the Year"). The four major Sabbats and their dates are: Imbolg or Candlemas (February 2), Beltane or May Day (May 1), Lughnasadh or Lammas (August 1), and Samhain or Halloween (October 31–November 1). The four minor Sabbats and their dates are: Spring Equinox or Ostara (approximately March 22), Summer Solstice or Midsummer (approximately June 21), Autumn Equinox or Mabon (approximately September 22), and Winter Solstice, Yule, or Midwinter (approximately December 22).

The following is a list of various precious stones and the Witches' Sabbats to which they correspond:

Gemstones of the Sabbats	
Imbolg (Candlemas)	Amethyst and Turquoise
Ostara (Spring Equinox)	Aquamarine, Jasper, Moonstone, and Rose Quartz
Beltane (May Day)	Bloodstone and Sapphire
Summer Solstice (Midsummer)	Diamond, Emerald, Jade, Lapis Lazuli, and Tiger's Eye
Lughnasadh (Lammas)	Citrine, Peridot, and Yellow Diamond
Mabon (Autumn Equinox)	Amethyst and Yellow Topaz
Samhain (Halloween)	Carnelian, Obsidian, and Onyx
Winter Solstice (Yule or Midwinter)	Bloodstone, Garnet, and Ruby

Sabbat gemstones can be worn in the form of jewelry and/ or placed on the altar to empower Sabbat rituals with the vital energies of Gaia. In addition, they can be used to mark off ritual circle space. Some Witches also use them when performing Sabbat divinations. For example, the scrying of an obsidian mirror or sphere at Samhain, or the use of a terminated rose quartz crystal as a dowsing pendulum at Spring Equinox.

> *"Imbolg was also the traditional time to collect stones for new magick circles and for general magickal use."*
>
> —Edain McCoy

Resources

The Blue Turtle

14 Prospect Street
Madison, New Jersey 07940
Phone: 973-377-0980
E-mail: theblueturtle@nac.net
Website: *www.theblueturtle.com*

The Crystal Ball Inc.

1918 East Capitol Drive
Shorewood, Wisconsin 53211
Phone: 414-967-8888 or 888-255-1175
E-mail: shop@wehug.com
Website: *www.wehug.com*

The Crystal Lady

PO Box 1597
Sulphur Springs, Texas 75482
E-mail: crystal@crystallady.com
Website: *www.crystallady.com*

Crystals of the Myst

77 Gallatin Street (or PO Box 508)
Buffalo, New York 14207
Phone/Fax: 716-875-9076
E-mail: info@crystalsofthemyst.com
Website: *www.crystalsofthemyst.com*

Dancing Moon

12315 Judson Road
San Antonio, Texas 78233
Phone: 210-946-6464
E-mail: dancingmoon@compuvision.net
Website: *www.dancing-moon.com*

Dave's Down to Earth Rock Shop *and* The Prehistoric Life Museum

704 Main Street
Evanston Illinois 60202
Phone: 847-866-7374
Fax: 847-866-6854
Website: *www.davesdowntoearthrockshop.com/index.htm*

Gary's Gem Garden

Sawmill Village Shopping Center
404 Route 70 East
Cherry Hill, New Jersey 08034
Phone: 856-795-5077
Fax: 856-795-0786
E-mail: info@garysgemgarden.com
Website: *garysgemgarden.com*

Golightly's Rock Shop

HCR 4–76B
Leon, Virginia 22725
Phone: 540-547-2714
Fax: 540-547-3258
E-mail: unakite@erols.com
Website: *www.jackgolightly.com/index.html*

Magickware

7657 Winnetka Avenue #102
Canoga Park, California 91306
Phone: 818-881-0827
E-mail: branwen@magickware.com
Website: *www.magickware.com/gemstones.html*

Mooncave Crystals

PMB 162
220 W. Cota Street
Shelton, Washington 98584
Phone: 360-432-2340
E-mail: mirabaimoon@earthlink.net
Website: *www.mooncavecrystals.com*

Mordaunte's Coffin Gems & Jewelry

4211 Killarney Court
Lansing, Michigan 48911
E-mail: mordaunte@coffingems.com
Website: *www.coffingems.com*

Multistone International Inc.

135 South Holliday Street
Strasburg, Virginia 22657
Phone: 540-465-8777
Fax: 540-465-8773
E-mail: info@multistoneintl.com
Website: *www.multistoneintl.com*

Mystic Merchant

Semmes, Alabama 36575
Phone: 251-645-9081
E-mail: mystic@mysticmerchant.com
Website: *www.mysticmerchant.com/index.html*

New Moon Occult Shop

PO Box 110
DIDCOT, Oxon OX11 9YT
United Kingdom
Contact: Rev. Judith Lewis
Phone (UK): 01235-819-744
Phone (US): 011-44-123-581-9744
Fax (UK): 01235-812-367
Fax (US): 011-44-123-581-2367
E-mail: sales@new-moon.demon.co.uk
Website: *www.newmoonoccultshop.com*

The Old Age Metaphysical Country Store

7152 Alabama Avenue
Canoga Park, California 91303
Phone: 818-883-7115
Website: *www.metaphysical-store.com*

Panpipes Magickal Marketplace

1641 Cahuenga Boulevard
Hollywood, California 90028
Phone: 323-462-7078
Fax: 323-462-6700
E-mail: info@panpipes.com
Website: *www.panpipes.com*

Sanctuary Crystals

5524 Cal Sag Road (Route 83)
Alsip, Illinois 60803
Phone: 708-396-2833
E-mail: sanctuary@ync.net
Website: *www.sanctuarycrystals.com/index.htm*

South Pacific Wholesale Company

114 River Street
Montpelier, Vermont 05602
Phone: 800-338-2162
E-mail: mail@southpacificwholesale.com
Website: *www.beading.com/catalogue.html*

Stone Age

2-4 High Street
Glastonbury BA6 9DU
United Kingdom
Phone: 014580-835-514
E-mail: crystals@stoneage.co.uk
Website: *www.stoneage.co.uk/acatalog*

Thought and Memory

Crystal and Gemstone Skulls
Email: ravenia@thoughtandmemory.com
Website: *www.thoughtandmemory.com*

Bibliography

Agrippa, Henry Cornelius. *The Philosophy of Natural Magic.* (Originally published in 1531). Reprint. Secaucus, N.J.: University Books, 1974.

Banis, Victor. *Charms, Spells and Curses for the Millions.* Los Angeles, Calif.: Sherbourne Press, 1970.

Barrett, Francis. *The Magus, or Celestial Intelligencer.* (Originally published in London in 1801.) Reprint. New York: University Books, 1967.

Best, Michael R. and Frank H. Brightman. *The Book of Secrets of Albertus Magnus, or the Virtues of Herbs, Stones and Certain Beasts.* London: Oxford University Press, 1973.

Brand, John and Sir Henry Ellis. *Observations on Popular Antiquities.* London: Chatto and Windus, 1877.

Bowes, Susan. *Notions and Potions.* New York: Sterling Publishing Company, Inc., 1997.

Budge, E. A. Wallis. *Amulets and Superstitions.* (Originally published by Oxford University Press, London, in 1930.) New York: Dover Publications, Inc., 1978.

Cavendish, Richard. *The Black Arts*. New York: Perigee Books, 1983.

Chase, Pamela Louise and Jonathan Pawlik. *Healing With Gemstones*. Franklin Lakes, N.J.: New Page Books, 2002.

Crow, W. B. *Precious Stones: Their Occult Power and Hidden Significance*. London: Aquarian Press, 1970.

Crowley, Aleister. *777 and Other Qabalistic Writings of Aleister Crowley*. York Beach, Maine: Weiser Books, 1986.

Bels. "The Koh-i-noor Diamond." 23 Jan 2003. < http://www.bbc.co.uk/dna/h2g2/alabaster/A730801>.

"The Blue Hope." 24 Jan 2003 < http://www.williamsdiamond.com/famousdiamonds.html>.

Cunningham, Scott. *Cunningham's Encyclopedia of Crystal, Gem and Metal Magic*. Saint Paul, Minn.: Llewellyn Publications, 1988.

de Courcy, Anne. "Diamond Lore—The Koh-i-Noor." 23 Jan 2003 http://brysonburke.com/lore_kohinoor.html>.

Evans, Joan. *Magical Jewels of the Middle Ages and the Renaissance*. (Originally published in 1922.) Reprint. New York: Dover, 1976.

Fernie, William Thomas. *The Occult and Curative Powers of Precious Stones*. New York: Rudolf Steiner Publications, 1973. (Originally published in England in 1907 under the title: *Precious Stones for Curative Wear and Other Remedial Uses; Likewise the Nobler Metals*.)

Fowler, Marian. *Hope: Adventures of a Diamond*. Toronto, Canada: Random House Canada, 2002.

Frazer, James. *The Golden Bough: A Study in Magic and Religion*. New York: Macmillan, 1956.

Gardner, Joy. *Color and Crystals: A Journey Through the Chakras*. Freedom, Calif.: The Crossing Press, 1988.

Ghosn, M. T. *The Origin of Birthstones and Stone Legends.* Lomita, Calif.: Inglewood Lapidary, 1984.

Gibson, Walter B. and Litzka R. *The Complete Illustrated Book of the Psychic Sciences.* Garden City, N.Y.: Doubleday and Company, Inc., 1966.

Giles, Carl H. and Barbara Ann Williams. *Bewitching Jewelry: Jewelry of the Black Art.* Cranbury, N.J.: A. S. Barnes, 1976.

Gonzales-Wippler, Migene. *The Complete Book of Amulets and Talismans.* Saint Paul, Minn.: Llewellyn Publications, 1997.

Gray, Eden. *A Complete Guide to the Tarot.* New York: Bantam Books, 1970.

Gray, Eden. *Mastering the Tarot.* New York: Signet, 1971.

Greer, John Michael. *Natural Magic: Potions and Powers from the Magical Garden.* Saint Paul, Minn.: Llewellyn Publications, 2000.

Guiley, Rosemary Ellen. *The Encyclopedia of Witches and Witchcraft.* New York: Facts on File, 1989.

Guiley, Rosemary Ellen. *Harper's Encyclopedia of Mystical and Paranormal Experience.* New York: HaperCollins Publishers, 1991.

Heiniger, Earnst A. and Jean. *Great Book of Jewels.* Boston, Mass.: New York Graphic Society, 1974.

Holland, Eileen. *The Wicca Handbook.* York Beach, Maine: Samuel Weiser, Inc., 2000.

Jordan, Michael. *Encyclopedia of Gods.* New York: Facts on File, 1993.

Kapoor, Gouri Shanker. *Gems and Astrology: A Guide to Health, Happiness and Prosperity.* New Delhi, India: Ranjan Publications, 1985.

Kunz, George Frederick. *The Curious Lore of Precious Stones.* (Originally published in 1913.) Reprint. New York: Dover, 1977.

Leach, Maria, editor. *Standard Dictionary of Folklore, Mythology and Legend.* New York: Funk and Wagnalls, 1972.

Leek, Sybil. *The Sybil Leek Book of Fortune Telling.* Toronto, Ontario: Collier-Macmillan Canada Ltd., 1969.

Llewellyn's 1995 Magical Almanac. Saint Paul, Minn.: Llewellyn Publications, 1994.

Magic Charms From A to Z. Middletown, R.I.: The Witches' Almanac, Ltd., 1999.

McCoy, Edain. *The Sabbats: A New Approach to Living the Old Ways.* Saint Paul, Minn.: Llewellyn Publications, 1996.

Mella, Dorothee L. *Stone Power: The Legendary and Practical Use of Gems and Stones.* Albuquerque, N.M.: Domel, 1976.

Melody. *Love is in the Earth: A Kaleidoscope of Crystals.* Wheat Ridge, Colo.: Earth-Love Publishing House, 1995.

Miller, Gustavus Hindman. *10,000 Dreams Interpreted.* Dorset, England: Element Books Limited, 1996.

Opie, Iona and Moira Tatem. *A Dictionary of Superstitions.* New York: Oxford University Press, 1989.

Parkinson, Cornelia M. Gem Magic: *The Wonder of Your Birthstone.* New York: Ballantine Books, 1988.

Pavitt, William. *The Book of Talismans, Amulets, and Zodiacal Gems.* (Originally published in 1914.) Reprint. North Hollywood, Calif.: Wilshire, 1970.

Petro, Robert and Andrea. *The Mystery of the Talking Stones.* Sedona, Ariz.: WindSpirit Productions, 1999.

Pickering, David. *The Cassell Dictionary of Superstitions.* London: Cassell, 1995.

Richardson, Wally and Jenny, and Lenora Huett. *Spiritual Value of Gem Stones*. Marina del Rey, Calif.: DeVorss and Company, 1980.

Savedow, Steve. *Goetic Evocation*. Chicago, Ill.: Eschaton Productions, 1996.

Savedow, Steve. *The Magician's Workbook: A Modern Grimoire*. York Beach, Maine: Samuel Weiser, Inc., 1995.

Shaw, Eva. *Divining the Future: Prognostication from Astrology to Zoomancy*. New York: Facts on File, Inc., 1995.

Silbey, Uma. *The Complete Crystal Guidebook*. New York: Bantam Books, 1986.

Simpson, Liz. *The Book of Crystal Healing*. New York: Sterling Publishing Company, Inc., 1997.

Stein, Diane. *All Women Are Healers: A Comprehensive Guide to Natural Healing*. Freedom, Calif.: The Crossing Press, 1990.

Stein, Diane. *The Women's Spirituality Book*. Saint Paul, Minn.: Llewellyn Publications, 1987.

Strange Stories, Amazing Facts. Pleasantville, N.Y.: Reader's Digest Association, Inc., 1976.

Sullivan, Kevin. *The Crystal Handbook*. New York: Signet, 1987.

Thomson, H. A. *Legends of Gems: Strange Beliefs Which the Astrological Birthstones Have Collected Through the Ages*. Los Angeles, Calif.: Graphic Press, 1937.

Uyldert, Mellie. *The Magic of Precious Stones*. Wellingborough, England: Turnstone Press, 1981.

Valiente, Doreen. *An ABC of Witchcraft Past and Present*. New York: Saint Martin's Press, 1973.

Villiers, Elizabeth. *The Book of Charms*. (Originally published in 1927.) Reprint. New York: Simon and Schuster, 1973.

Waite, Arthur Edward. *The Pictorial Key to the Tarot.* New York: Citadel Press, 1990.

Walker, Barbara G. *The Women's Encyclopedia of Myths and Secrets.* Edison, N.J.: Castle Books, 1996.

Wright, Elbee. *Book of Legendary Spells.* Minneapolis, Minn.: Marlar Publishing, 1974.

Ward, W. S. "The Koh-i-noor Diamond." 10 Jan 2003 <www.jewelryexpert.com/articles/Koh-i-noor-Diamond.htm>.

Index

About the Author

erina Dunwich is a High Priestess of the Old Religion, who has devoted many years of her life to studying, practicing, and writing about the magickal arts and occult sciences. She is the founder of the Pagan Poets Society and Golden Isis Press, and has authored numerous books on Witchcraft and Pagan lore. A tarot advisor, ordained minister, spiritualist medium, and cat lover, Dunwich currently resides in Southern California.

Other Books by Gerina Dunwich:

Candlelight Spells

The Magick of Candleburning
(republished as Wicca Candle Magick)

The Concise Lexicon of the Occult

Circle of Shadows

Wicca Craft

The Secrets of Love Magick
(republished as Wicca Love Spells)

The Wicca Spellbook

The Wicca Book of Days

The Wicca Garden

The Wicca Source Book

The Wicca Source Book, Revised Second Edition

The Modern Witch's Complete Source Book

Everyday Wicca

A Wiccan's Guide to Prophecy and Divination
(republished as The Wiccan's Dictionary of
Prophecy and Omens)

Wicca A to Z

Magick Potions

Your Magickal Cat

The Pagan Book of Halloween

Exploring Spellcraft

Herbal Magick

The Cauldron of Dreams

A Witches' Guide to Ghosts and the Supernatural

FREE INFORMATION - SPECIAL SAVINGS
Learn More About the Full Line of
Mind / Body / Spirit Titles from *New Page Books*

◻ Wicca ◻ Magickal Arts ◻ Herbalism ◻ Alternative Therapies ◻ Astrology
◻ Spellcraft ◻ Rituals ◻ Folk Magic ◻ Wellness ◻ Numerology
◻ Meditation ◻ Aromatherapy ◻ Candle Magick ◻ Visualization
◻ Healing ◻ Celts and Druids ◻ Shamanism ◻ Dream Interpretation ◻ Yoga
◻ Divination ◻ Tarot ◻ Palmistry ◻ Graphology ◻ Supernatural ◻ Gemstones
…and many more, by the authors you trust!

SELECTED TITLES INCLUDE:

◻ **Ancient Spellcraft** - Perry
◻ **Animal Spirit** -Telesco & Hall
◻ **Celebrating Wiccan Spirituality** - Lady Sabrina
◻ **Celtic Astrology** - Vega
◻ **Celtic Myth and Legend** - Squire
◻ **A Charmed Life** - Telesco
◻ **Circle of Isis** - Reed
◻ **Clan of the Goddess** - Brondwin
◻ **Creating Home Sanctuaries** - Mitchell w/Gunning
◻ **Crop Circles** - Andrews w/Spignesi
◻ **Dreams of the Goddess** - Ross
◻ **Dunwich's Guide to Gemstone Sorcery** - Dunwich
◻ **Earth Magic** - Weinstein
◻ **An Enchanted Life** - Telesco
◻ **Enchantments of the Heart** - Morrison
◻ **Exploring Candle Magick** - Telesco
◻ **Exploring Celtic Druidism** - Knight
◻ **Exploring Chakras** - Shumsky
◻ **Exploring Feng Shui** - Mitchell w/Gunning
◻ **Exploring Meditation** - Shumsky
◻ **Exploring Scrying** - Hawk
◻ **Exploring Spellcraft** - Dunwich
◻ **Exploring Wicca** - Lady Sabrina
◻ **Faery Magick** - Knight
◻ **Gardening with the Goddess** - Telesco

◻ **Handwriting Analysis** - Amend & Ruiz
◻ **Healing with Gemstones** - Chase & Pawlik
◻ **Herbal Magick** - Dunwich
◻ **Karmic Tarot, 3rd Ed.** - Lammey
◻ **Maiden Magick** - Brondwin
◻ **Mastering Candle Magick** - Telesco
◻ **The Miracle Tree** - Stewart
◻ **Pagans and the Law** - Eilers
◻ **Positive Magic** - Weinstein
◻ **The Practical Pagan** - Eilers
◻ **Raising Witches** - O'Gaea
◻ **Self-Hypnosis** - Goldberg
◻ **Star Power** - MacGregor
◻ **Tarot: A Classic Handbook for the Apprentice** - Connolly
◻ **Tarot: A New Handbook for the Apprentice** - Connolly
◻ **Tarot for Your Self, 2nd Ed.** - Greer
◻ **The Well-Read Witch** - McColman
◻ **When Someone You Love is Wiccan** - McColman
◻ **A Wiccan Bible** - Drew
◻ **Wicca for Couples** - Drew
◻ **Wicca Spellcraft for Men** - Drew
◻ **The Wiccan Wellness Book** - Perry
◻ **A Witch's Master Grimoire** - Lady Sabrina
◻ *and more!*

To be a member of our *New Page Books Club* – and receive our catalog, special savings, and advance notice on upcoming titles – send your name and address to the address listed below. Or for fast service, please call 1-800-227-3371 and give operator code 672 We look forward to hearing from you!

newpagebooks.com
Books subject to availability.

New Page Books
Dept. 672, 3 Tice Road
Franklin Lakes, NJ 07417